NECESSARY
NOISE

NECESSARY NOISE

HOW DONALD TRUMP INFLAMES THE CULTURE WAR AND WHY THIS IS GOOD NEWS FOR AMERICA

STAR PARKER
WITH RICHARD MANNING

CENTER
STREET

NEW YORK NASHVILLE

Center Street
Hachette Book Group
1290 Avenue of the Americas, New York, NY 10104
centerstreet.com
twitter.com/centerstreet

First Edition: November 2019

Center Street is a division of Hachette Book Group, Inc. The Center Street name and logo are trademarks of Hachette Book Group, Inc.

The publisher is not responsible for websites (or their content) that are not owned by the publisher.

The Hachette Speakers Bureau provides a wide range of authors for speaking events. To find out more, go to www.HachetteSpeakersBureau.com or call (866) 376-6591.

Library of Congress Cataloging-in-Publication Data has been applied for.

ISBNs: 978-1-5460-7658-2 (hardcover), 978-1-5460-7660-5 (ebook)

Printed in the United States of America

LSC-C

10 9 8 7 6 5 4 3 2 1

In memory of two of my most beloved mentors,
Dr. E. V. Hill and Pastor Ken Hutcherson,
both now in eternity after dedicating their lives to further God's
perspectives regarding culture, poverty, and race relations.
—Star Parker

To my Dad, who helped make me the man that I am. And my
wife, who always loves me, even when I don't.
—Richard Manning

Contents

Preface

TWO QUESTIONS had been stirring within me prior to the election of Donald J. Trump about the state of our country. I've been wrestling with these two questions since I entered the political and public discussion world some twenty-five years ago. I'd been writing about and talking about issues surrounding these questions through more than a thousand nationally syndicated columns, four books, more than 250 college or university speeches, and countless television and radio appearances on shows from *Oprah* and *The View* to those featuring Rush Limbaugh, Sean Hannity, and James Dobson as well as C-SPAN. One deals with our culture, and one deals with our economy.

The first question was whether America's culture war would turn into physical war. America had been at war with herself between the interests of the left and the interests of the right for the last fifty years. We had become a nation where politicians were passing laws to teach children and grandchildren values inconsistent with those of their parents. We had arrived at a place where judges were redefining truth and changing the culture by edict. This war was for the very heart and soul of our country and had been intensifying.

The second question was whether America would move away from its federal government intervening into every aspect of the economy so that innovation and individual initiative would be allowed to flourish. The great struggle we've been having between capitalism and socialism had been costly. We had reached a dangerous mass of special interests: they had too much stake in big government, whether they were employed by it, were collecting benefits from it, or were businesses getting favors from it. And the emotional and economic costs of government overreach were taking a toll on all of us as neighbors.

At the core of this were two questions: Would America be a society that is biblical and free? Or a society that is secular and statist?

Under normal circumstances, Americans would battle in the voting booth to elect our government bodies that determine our laws and set public policy regarding which direction our society would take. Once the voting was over, we'd settle into the results and prepare for the next election.

But this time the circumstances were not normal.

The presidential election of 2016 left many in our country reeling and dumbfounded with the outcome, which would inaugurate Donald Trump as the forty-fifth President of the United States of America. I was one of those dealing with a mix of emotion—surprise, concern, uncertainty—about what his presidency would mean for our nation both in the short term and in the decades to come. But now that Donald Trump is well into his first term, I am more convinced than ever that his devout and initial supporters had it right and that he was the very president America needed to get our country back on course toward its founding principles.

Yet concerns prior to his election were also legitimate. How would this business leader with no prior governmental experience lead our nation? Could such a divisive campaign bring a divided country together and help it? How would his unrepented and immoral sexual background affect U.S. culture and expectations for its leadership?

After these visceral reactions that immediately followed the election, a realization hit me as I listened to President Trump's first speech as the leader of our country: that there may have been a silver lining to his unexpected presidency. By the incredible increase of debate, confusion, and angst that occupied everything from TV news talk shows and radio airwaves to social media and private conversations, a door may have been opened wide for America to finally and meaningfully discuss her problems.

The noise of current debate can seem deafening and senseless, but just as a marriage counselor would advise that a healthy marriage demands open hearts and honest dialogue, so too our country needs the honest and candid dialogue of her people. Trump's election provides us with an opportunity like never before to engage with each other in this way.

Living and working in Washington, D.C., I am only a six-block stroll from my apartment to my office. This walk takes me down what is called the "Lincoln Legacy," where I pass Ford's Theatre where President Lincoln was shot and the Petersen House where he died.

Since Trump's election, every time I walk by these places, I think about the noise that led to the Civil War. There was a major question in the country at that time that needed to be addressed, and the nation could no longer continue to ignore it. I think about the intensity of the debate and the emotional investments on both sides of that culture war. The series of Lincoln–Douglas debates in 1858 clarified the sides and moved the nation to choose one. I marvel at how the Trump presidency has forced similar clarifications of the two sides and moved the needle for intense discussion to the front and center of our society. Yes, there is no need to deny that the election of President Donald Trump came with noise. America now had a president who understood that our nation was going in the wrong direction from her founding principles and that most Americans on the left scorn our founders. America now had a president who understood the dangers of multiculturalism, and his discussions about American exceptionalism were unnerving the diversity clan. America now had a president who understood the virtues of business and how excessive taxation and regulation stymied growth and stagnated the economy, which is antithetical to democratic socialists.

But I think the noise is necessary to make America wholesome and whole, and frankly I believe that the louder the noise gets, the better off we will be as Americans. As Lincoln pointed out in his famous House Divided Speech in 1858, our nation could no longer be half free and half slave; our nation would "become all one thing, or all the other," but no longer could we be both.

I've written *Necessary Noise* so that:

1. You will better understand the greatest threats to America's foundational values and prosperity;
2. You will better understand the unique ways Trump's presidency is working to restore our culture and protect our future; and
3. You will be encouraged to join the debate and you will have more tools to engage in meaningful and rational discussions with others to broaden the expansion of thought.

In writing this book, I have taken a look at some of the data related to our current political and social environment to help us deal with the challenges and contentions that culminated in the election and inauguration of Donald Trump.

I hope you will read *Necessary Noise* with an open mind as I explore how the roller-coaster ride we're on is not only aggressively noisy but uncomfortably necessary for cultural clarity and ultimately for our nation's future.

I hope that you will trust me when I say the noise has purpose. That without the presidency of Donald Trump, our country would not be debating the hard issues we are forced to deal with now.

For the passionate Trump supporter, I hope *Necessary Noise* will move you beyond a purely reactionary position regarding the specific issue or two that motivated you to campaign hard for him to be elected and that you will be patient with others who may still not see what you see or know what you know. We didn't get on the wrong course yesterday, so we cannot turn the ship around tomorrow. I thank God that you knew what you knew and saw what you saw before the *Titanic* hit the iceberg. For individuals still stunned by the

Trump presidency, I hope *Necessary Noise* will help you understand how the frustrations of our country reached such a breaking point—particularly in the Midwest where most Americans in our smaller and heartland communities try every day to live by the rules and do right by their family and neighbors only to wake up one day furious that our nation had spiraled into debauchery, collectivism, and political correctness, and that far too many fellow Americans had devolved into moral relativism and government dependency. Perhaps upon reading this book you will indulge the unique opportunities that can result after a major argument for America to recapture its moral high ground both spiritually and economically through the disruptive Donald Trump. And for others, I think *Necessary Noise* will help you understand the *why* for Trump enthusiasm, whether you like it or not.

Introduction

IT IS AS NOISY in Washington, D.C., as it is in the rest of our nation, where much debate is being had about who we are supposed to be as a country, how we got off track from our founding principles, and what can be done if anything to fix ourselves.

Upon the election of President Donald Trump, the five noisiest places inside the Beltway became the White House; Congress; the media; K Street, which headquarters many of D.C.'s most prestigious lobby firms; and the policy idea world, the world in which I work.

I knew it was getting really loud in the public square and that the noise would eventually spill into a possible reset for our society because as a social activist, media commentator, and syndicated columnist I had been noticing for years that people in the heartland of America were becoming extremely divided in their worldviews and that decent folks in our quiet communities were growing very nervous about our government being overrun with career legislators, lobbyists, and lawyers. The folks invested in the comfort zone of our country's capital were very nervous when Trump won the election because he campaigned on a promise to drain the swamp. He ran on a promise to disrupt the status quo in Washington, D.C.

Over the past twenty years, lecture travels and my work through my organization, the Center for Urban Renewal and Education

(CURE), a D.C.-based policy institute that addresses issues of culture, poverty, and race relations, have taken me to every state in the union. I've known and have been saying for years that we had reached a critical crossroads between the worldviews of the left and the right. The great divide between those who believed in limited government, individual merit, and biblical morality and those who believed in situational ethics, redistribution, and big government was diminishing our national morale and forcing our public square to become a battleground of constant conflict.

Many conservative social warriors, writers, and commentators had attempted to discuss with America that every institution ensuring an environment for self-governance—religion, family, education, commerce, and local governance—was under attack; or, as many liberals might describe it, was being *transformed*. But these warnings continued to fall upon deaf ears, and over time our U.S. Supreme Court moved into becoming the most powerful institution in our country.

When Mitt Romney ran for president against incumbent Barack Obama he stumbled into this cultural debate when caught on tape at a fundraiser in Florida saying that 47 percent of Americans were dependent on government and therefore he didn't expect many votes from them. Romney was mocked in the media, with some pundits concluding that that comment cost Romney the presidency, but the point he was trying to make was accurate.

All social snapshots up until that moment were clear that not only was the large, chronically poor portion of our population dependent on government creating insurmountable problems in our most distressed communities, but there was compelling research that dependence on government influences cultural shifts toward secularism and socialism.

And we had been going off track toward the leftist utopia of a "transformed" America for a long time.

Our nation began with the foundation of eternal truths and personal responsibility, with governing principles rooted in biblical values, a limited role of government to simply protect individual initiative and interests, free and open markets for capitalism and profits, and "e pluribus unum," or "out of many, one."

America was the first such nation in the history of the world. For those who need a refresher course, the British preferred big government controls over the colonies of the New World; the people of the New World preferred freedom and fair taxation, so they rebelled; a war was fought; the Brits lost; and the United States was birthed. The founders of this new nation then drafted a Declaration of Independence and a Constitution, which embodied the four governing principles I listed above.

In the generations that followed, where there were errors made or actions that proved to oppose our founding principles, the American people self-corrected. In one instance, a civil war resulted. In another instance, America changed course regarding the civil rights movement and expounded its constitutional protections for blacks.

Forty-five years after the Civil Rights Act was signed into law and one year into the election of President Barack Obama, very different and difficult questions beyond race and racial atonement from America's past began to surface. Many Americans both black and white had voted for Obama with hope that the race tensions in America would once again and forever be settled. After the very bloody and broad race riots of the late sixties, most Americans both white and black wanted a truce and some peace. Relationships across racial lines began to build slowly but strongly over the four decades that proceeded the civil rights movement. Yet while whites and blacks were learning to work together, play together, and live as neighbors, the country was starting to divide into red and blue states to reflect the worldviews of the two sides of the culture war. The abortion debate was raging with no end in sight, and taxes were rising more and more, with the burden falling more and more on the average family.

When candidate Obama ran on a message of hope and change, the majority of Americans both white and black got excited. A great recession as a result of a burst housing bubble and a prolonged war as a result of 9/11 had taken a toll, so his message rung into hurting hearts like Sunday morning church bells. Yet soon into the Obama presidency, the beautiful symphony turned into left-wing clanging, and our nation rapidly slid into race consciousness unseen since the era of Jim Crow ended.

In 2010, the heartland of America started asking itself what was happening. How did hard work and profit succumb to political whims of redistribution under the guise of social justice? How did Christ become the villain of civil society when it was this religious philosophy that ended slavery, polygamy, and caste systems by promoting messages of individual uniqueness, capacity, and brilliance?

As a Christian conservative observing the biblical mandate that a soft answer turns away wrath, I was a bit dismayed by the political groundswell that rallied Donald Trump for the Republican nomination, and I wrote about my concerns in a few of my weekly nationally syndicated columns. I was all in for Senator Ted Cruz throughout most of the primaries and heard loudly from Trump supporters every time I wrote about my support. At the point of the Billy Bush tapes, I went as far as to opine that he should move over for Mike Pence.

But as Trump had emerged as the nominee by berating and then beating all sixteen of his Republican opponents one by one and was now going to surf above the wave of such crass talk, I began to think that maybe Donald Trump was more than a reflection of America's secular, sensational, and sassy side. Perhaps he was the big brother needed to rescue a marginalized, fearful, and weakened Christian church and community that was losing on every front of the culture war.

In fact, I concluded after he won and before his inauguration that his election was fulfillment of Proverbs 21:1, that the heart of man is in God's hand and "like the rivers of water He turns it wherever He wishes." That He determines: and in this case, God had chosen not only to exasperate and provoke but also to exacerbate and accelerate America's culture war.

On January 20, 2017, Donald J. Trump came into Washington, D.C., raised his right hand, put his left hand on a Bible, and was sworn into the office of the President.

I was present on that day to experience him address the nation and the world as America's newly elected forty-fifth president.

Here's what he said:

We, the citizens of America, are now joined in a great national effort to rebuild our country and to restore its promise for all of our people. Together, we will determine the course of America and the world for years to come.

We will face challenges. We will confront hardships. But we will get the job done.

Every four years, we gather on these steps to carry out the orderly and peaceful transfer of power, and we are grateful to President Obama and First Lady Michelle Obama for their gracious aid throughout this transition. They have been magnificent.

Today's ceremony, however, has very special meaning. Because today we are not merely transferring power from one administration to another, or from one party to another—but we are transferring power from Washington, D.C., and giving it back to you, the American people.

For too long, a small group in our nation's capital has reaped the rewards of government while the people have borne the cost.

Washington flourished—but the people did not share in its wealth. Politicians prospered—but the jobs left, and the factories closed. The establishment protected itself, but not the citizens of our country.

Their victories have not been your victories; their triumphs have not been your triumphs; and while they celebrated in our nation's capital, there was little to celebrate for struggling families all across our land.

That all changes—starting right here, and right now, because this moment is your moment: it belongs to you.

It belongs to everyone gathered here today and everyone watching all across America. This is your day. This is your celebration. And this, the United States of America, is your country.

What truly matters is not which party controls our government, but whether our government is controlled by the people.

January 20th 2017, will be remembered as the day the people became the rulers of this nation again. The forgotten men and women of our country will be forgotten no longer. Everyone is listening to you now.

You came by the tens of millions to become part of a historic movement the likes of which the world has never seen before. At the center of this movement is a crucial conviction: that a nation exists to serve its citizens.

Americans want great schools for their children, safe neighborhoods for their families, and good jobs for themselves. These are the just and reasonable demands of a righteous public.

But for too many of our citizens, a different reality exists: Mothers and children trapped in poverty in our inner cities; rusted-out factories scattered like tombstones across the landscape of our nation; an education system, flush with cash, but which leaves our young and beautiful students deprived of knowledge; and the crime and gangs and drugs that have stolen too many lives and robbed our country of so much unrealized potential. This American carnage stops right here and stops right now.

We are one nation—and their pain is our pain. Their dreams are our dreams; and their success will be our success. We share one heart, one home, and one glorious destiny. The oath of office I take today is an oath of allegiance to all Americans.

For many decades, we've enriched foreign industry at the expense of American industry; subsidized the armies of other countries while allowing for the very sad depletion of our military; we've defended other nation's borders while refusing to defend our own; and spent trillions of dollars overseas while America's infrastructure has fallen into disrepair and decay.

We've made other countries rich while the wealth, strength, and confidence of our country has disappeared over the horizon. One by one, the factories shuttered and left our shores, with not even a thought about the millions upon millions of American workers left behind.

The wealth of our middle class has been ripped from their homes and then redistributed across the entire world. But that is the past. And now we are looking only to the future.

We assembled here today are issuing a new decree to be heard in every city, in every foreign capital, and in every hall of power. From this day forward, a new vision will govern our land. From this moment on, it's going to be America First.

Every decision on trade, on taxes, on immigration, on foreign affairs, will be made to benefit American workers and American families.

We must protect our borders from the ravages of other countries making our products, stealing our companies, and destroying our jobs. Protection will lead to great prosperity and strength.

I will fight for you with every breath in my body—and I will never, ever let you down. America will start winning again, winning like never before.

We will bring back our jobs. We will bring back our borders. We will bring back our wealth. And we will bring back our dreams.

We will build new roads, and highways, and bridges, and airports, and tunnels, and railways all across our wonderful nation. We will get our people off of welfare and back to work—rebuilding our country with American hands and American labor. We will follow two simple rules: Buy American and hire American.

We will seek friendship and goodwill with the nations of the world—but we do so with the understanding that it is the right of all nations to put their own interests first. We do not seek to impose our way of life on anyone, but rather to let it shine as an example for everyone to follow.

We will reinforce old alliances and form new ones—and unite the civilized world against radical Islamic terrorism, which we will eradicate completely from the face of the Earth.

At the bedrock of our politics will be a total allegiance to the United States of America, and through our loyalty to our country, we will rediscover our loyalty to each other.

When you open your heart to patriotism, there is no room for prejudice.

The Bible tells us, "How good and pleasant it is when God's people live together in unity." We must speak our minds openly, debate our disagreements honestly, but always pursue solidarity.

When America is united, America is totally unstoppable. There should be no fear—we are protected, and we will always be protected.

We will be protected by the great men and women of our military and law enforcement and, most importantly, we are protected by God.

Finally, we must think big and dream even bigger.

In America, we understand that a nation is only living as long as it is striving. We will no longer accept politicians who are all talk and no action—constantly complaining but never doing anything about it. The time for empty talk is over. Now arrives the hour of action.

Do not let anyone tell you it cannot be done. No challenge can match the heart and fight and spirit of America. We will not fail. Our country will thrive and prosper again.

We stand at the birth of a new millennium, ready to unlock the mysteries of space, to free the Earth from the miseries of disease, and to harness the energies, industries and technologies of tomorrow.

A new national pride will stir our souls, lift our sights, and heal our divisions. It is time to remember that old wisdom our soldiers will never forget: that whether we are black or brown or white, we all bleed the same red blood of patriots, we all enjoy the same glorious freedoms, and we all salute the same great American Flag.

And whether a child is born in the urban sprawl of Detroit or the windswept plains of Nebraska, they look up at the same night sky, they fill their heart with the same dreams, and they are infused with the breath of life by the same almighty Creator.

So, to all Americans, in every city near and far, small and large, from mountain to mountain, and from ocean to ocean, hear these words: You will never be ignored again. Your voice, your hopes, and your dreams will define our American destiny. And your courage and goodness and love will forever guide us along the way.

Together, we will make America strong again. We will make America wealthy again. We will make America proud again. We will make America safe again. And yes, together, we will make America great again.

Thank you. God bless you. And God bless America.

The moment his inaugural speech concluded I felt fully confident that my instincts regarding his election were on point. I was fully persuaded that Donald Trump was a divine appointment and exactly what America needed to help fix her problems. I was deeply moved by his words, profoundly excited, and I was deeply energized that America had been extended providential mercy to course-correct toward her founding principles as a result of his presidency.

I predicted then, and it's been confirmed during his term, that President Trump was elected to peel back the political correctness in politics and in the media that had either hidden or stifled all discussions about the unraveling of our common culture. Discussions about America— who we are now, who we should be, and why this clarity matters.

I'd known for thirty years that we were in a raging culture war against the heart and soul of our most core and fundamental principles, and, just as in the 1850s, bitter tensions were escalating. Our country was literally splitting in half. Yet very few in leadership would even talk about it.

That's when I resolved to set aside any difference I may have had with the Trump persona, peculiarities, or temperament and do all I could within my sphere to help his administration be successful in every area of mutual agreement. In particular, fixing our inner cities, which cannot be done without addressing head-on my two questions on the culture war.

President Trump came into office with big bold promises. Immediately the venomous progressive political and media noise began.

The monsters of the swamp, so to speak, began to salivate and show fangs as a vicious serpent backed into a corner against a man ready to exercise his full intellectual and narcissistic capacity. Obama had a pen and a phone. Ha! Trump had attitude and Twitter.

The immediate noise of his opponents set the tone of intensity for the debates to come over some very serious questions, so I expected that things would get contentious, much more forceful, and much noisier. And they have.

Part of the tension is because America has been at a cultural crossroads with lots of fighting over whether her public square would be biblical and free or secular and statist.

I think our country broke down because our culture broke down, and our culture broke down because our classrooms broke down. Our classrooms broke down because our courts are broken, and our courts are broken because our Congress is no longer of, for, nor by the people but have become creatures of a swamp—swamp creatures who act as though they believe they are almighty and untouchable.

I believe Donald Trump is supported by a groundswell of decent people, from the quieter parts of our country known as the heartland who are saying that "enough is enough." People who get up and go to church on Sunday morning and to work on Monday morning. People who try to make proper choices for themselves and for their families. People who teach their children right from wrong according to biblical rules. People who then one day woke up and looked outside, saw utter chaos, and began to ask, "What has happened to my country?" Those supporters know that he is just getting started, they are perturbed by the distractions to get him off his agenda, and they are more energized than ever to keep him motivated and focused on his campaign promises.

Necessary Noise will shine a bright light on our raging debate regarding the direction for America's future. It will unveil Donald Trump's role in navigating the choppy waters to help determine if the three

Cs of her founding—Christianity, capitalism, and Constitution—will survive, and overcome the crassness, covetousness, and class warfare that could be her new national normal.

There is great and steadfast zeal among Trump supporters who believe that his election is the last chance to rescue our still young yet vulnerable nation from a moral and meaningless abyss. *Necessary Noise* will explore their concerns and will assess whether their hypothesis is correct—that the presidency of Donald Trump has turned the future of America toward the good.

PART ONE

SWAMP NOISE

CHAPTER ONE

Thank You, President Obama

T HEY SAY that a frog will boil to death if the temperature in a pot is gradually increased, but if there is a sudden increase in the heat, the frog will jump out of its once-cozy bath with no harm done.

America owes President Barack Obama a huge thank-you for turning up the heat under the pot of our cultural war. His big smile and boyhood charm were like warm water that deceived people into believing that his values were consistent with America's founding values. His entry onto the national political stage was grand. Beautiful everything. Humble beginnings, great marriage, adorable children, and vibrant promises that it was going to be a bright new day of hope and change in America.

Yet rapidly into his presidency, the prince evolved into a progressive. Concerns about government overreach, particularly on the issue of health care, began to emerge from various corners of our country. Folks who had voted for him were beginning to express buyer's remorse. Many then started putting together different aspects of various cultural battles only to discover that he was a wolf in sheep's clothing, a part of the liberal onslaught that had been working to destroy America's founding principles in every institution.

For some, concerns emerged when only seven months into his presidency, the illusion of Obama being a post-racial symbol for America was cracked after a Cambridge, Massachusetts, police officer arrested a Harvard professor for disorderly conduct while investigating a reported break-in at the professor's home. The facts of the case are yet unclear, it was the president's knee-jerk assumption that the police officer was likely wrong that shocked many who had hoped our nation's racial wounds were finally healing.

There was shock being articulated on radio talk show after talk show to have witnessed a president of the United States bowing to foreign potentates while apologizing for our nation's role in the world. It just wasn't sitting right with a lot of folks that his first speech abroad was in Cairo, Egypt, where he opened with remarks about "colonialism that denied rights and opportunities to many Muslims, and a Cold War in which Muslim-majority countries were too often treated as proxies without regard to their own aspirations." America at that point was still heavily at war in both Iraq and Afghanistan and only eight years from 9/11.

Another unsettling moment in his approach to foreign policy came in 2015 at the National Prayer Breakfast held annually in Washington, D.C., President Obama upbraided the audience about the Crusades. I was in attendance, and, yes, it was extremely uncomfortable. I said on *Hannity* the next day that sitting there taking his rebuke of Christianity was like verbal rape; I didn't consent to it, and it was brutal to endure.

We were exposed to horrific pictures of Middle Eastern Christians being beheaded, crucified, burned alive, or drowned in Egypt: just two weeks after his Prayer Breakfast speech. The horror of Islamic fascism was opened for all to see, only to be met by a flaccid response from Obama, which left many suspicious of his loyalties and increased their concerns for Israel, a high priority for evangelical Christians.

For others, patience in the warm pot was waning because of the decision by the Obama Justice Department to refuse to defend in federal court the Defense of Marriage Act of 1996 (known as DOMA) after candidate Obama had unequivocally stated during his presidential campaign that he supported the traditional view of marriage as being between a man and a woman. The tipping point for some trying to enthusiastically remain Obama supporters was this seemingly overnight collapse of his view on traditional marriage. He was elected on a platform of assurance that he fully supported conjugal marriage yet flip-flopped that position at the first opportunity.

The list of Obama offenses was growing long. Various pockets of voters both secular and sacred were adding up the inconsistencies and broken promises of his leadership. From his Justice Department brokering for firearms to be sold to people who fronted for Mexican drug cartels in order to trace the flow of these guns back into the United States to the news spin regarding the attack on American diplomats in Benghazi, Libya, tensions were building in the heartland that they had elected the wrong leader.

The stunning revelation that the Tucson and Phoenix offices of the Bureau of Alcohol, Tobacco, Firearms, and Explosives had decided to become suppliers of guns to the cartels through their Fast and Furious operation was tragically punctuated by a cartel member using one of those guns to murder Border Patrol Agent Brian Kelly.

The fake news story of the Democrats and the media that the September 11, 2012, terrorist attack was provoked by a very bad YouTube video that cost four American lives—Ambassador Christopher Steele and U.S. Foreign Services officer Sean Smith along with Tyrone Woods and Glen Doherty who were heroically trying to save them—insulted America's intelligence, but more importantly for many, it excused the attack itself as justified.

The failure to make legitimate rescue attempts when we learned later that resources were at the ready chilled those who had assumed that their military could always be trusted to act to protect their own and assaulted national pride in the fact that Americans leave no one behind. The pictures of the U.S. ambassador being dragged through the streets and the Obama administration's impotent reaction woke many of the frogs that had dosed in the pot.

Another eye-opening event for which to thank President Obama was when we learned that a formerly nameless, faceless bureaucrat at the Internal Revenue Service was weaponizing the tax collection agency to target Tea Party groups as well as conservative donors prior to the 2012 presidential elections to slow the discontentment growing in the heartland against the Obama administration.

Adding to this discontentment was then-Speaker Nancy Pelosi's famous 2010 Obamacare line "We have to pass it before you can read it," former Obama Chief of Staff Rahm Emanuel's "never let a good crisis go to waste," and even Obama's promise to "fundamentally transform America." When outright cynicism and contempt for the American people were laid bare, a decision was made to take back the country.

Prior to these back-to-back onslaughts of the Obama administration, most Americans operated on the assumption that politics was something that political people did and their getting involved didn't matter. They did their civic duty to vote most cycles and then trusted their elected officials to take care of the affairs of the country. They trusted that their elected officials knew and cared about the fundamentals of our founding principles.

So while heartland Americans were busy with the day-to-day business of their lives, a left-wing liberal progressive movement was fomenting transformation and had been working on this transformation inside education, entertainment, public policy, and the courts to entrench its left-wing liberal progressive domestic and foreign agenda and move it into the American mainstream.

But President Obama and his fellow left-wing liberal progressive (what from here on in I will refer to as LWLP) travelers made a big mistake. They overplayed their hand during his eight years in office by turning up the heat on the culture war. They believed that the American people had sedated into a coma in the boiling pot so their transformation mission could be sped up. They became aggressively boisterous, aggressively boastful, and aggressively brash. And their noise woke America up.

FIGHTING THE HEAT

First, they gave Republicans a congressional landslide in 2010; then after the anemic Romney lost in 2012, they gave House Republicans their largest majority since 1928, and in 2014, Republicans gained control of the U.S. Senate.

But the frog couldn't get out of the pot, even as Americans were screaming for a lifeline to escape, because in spite of these ballot-box wins, the pot was deep, dark, and filled with slimy swamp water.

The GOP leaders who claimed to care about freedom and liberty for the frog seemed to approach every dealing with Obama with fear in their eyes and the rationalization that fighting the corruption of everything was a political loser because it would require dramatic actions that they would be blamed for in the pages of the *Washington Post* or the *New York Times* or the editorial page of their local newspaper.

Their campaign brochures promised one thing, but in many cases they acclimated to the Beltway swamp tub, becoming beholden to Beltway journalists and lobbyists.

The fear of fighting an all-out war for what these elected officials may have at least once pretended to believe wasn't deemed worth the risk of losing a seat in the swamp. So many resolved to just use their positions to help lower the temperature under the boiling pot until after their reelection. They had become more dependent on the opinions of their donors than the opinions of their voters, so it became the case that donors were just paying for access while the politicians were just lying to their constituents back home.

Republican voters were assured that Obamacare would be repealed, but then after Senators Ted Cruz and Mike Lee and Representative Tom Graves actually tried to keep the GOP promise of repeal they were vilified internally for the 2013 defund fight, and anger in the grass roots began to rise. The new promise was that GOP leaders would get to it for real after they got control of the Senate.

The newly elected Republicans in Congress promised that they would use the power of the purse to get Obama spending under control as all Democrats were in lockstep fear of the political backlash. It was a tumultuous time of anxiety for heartland voters as on top of already-sluggish job recovery where a sixth of the American economy had collapsed under Obamacare. Instead, these Republican legislators just sat back and watched as his pen and phone continued to assault everything. Every substantive industry and institution was feeling the heat of his administration from inside the energy industry of coal and oil to the housing and banking industries and even to the point of his Education Department bureaucrats suing an Illinois school district to force it to allow high school boys to shower with girls.[1]

After eight years of the Obama administration, the LWLP control of the roller-coaster ride of our culture war was coming to a head. If not for President Barack Obama turning up the heat, the frog may have remained in the pot and died. So, thank you, Barack Obama, because had you not awakened the frog, a standard-issue Republican would have faced Hillary Clinton, and—win or lose—the three founding Cs of America would have remained under attack with only some tinkering around the edges.

Enter a brash, billionaire real estate developer and television star to pillar his sixteen befuddled Republican challengers. Donald Trump didn't talk the way politicians talked; offering few flowery words, Trump instead sent arrows to the heart of the problem time and again.

"They're bringing drugs. They're bringing crime. They're rapists," he said of border jumpers in the summer of 2015 when it was clear he was forming a presidential campaign for 2016. "Why can't we say, 'Merry Christmas'?" he asked of American churchgoers in the fall of 2015 while in Iowa, the opening state of presidential elections. "What the hell do you have to lose?" he demanded of blacks at a rally in Michigan in August 2016, three months before voters would make their decision for who would follow Barack Obama as the forty-fifth president of the United States of America.

It was clear to many who were comfortable inside the Beltway that Donald Trump was a man with a mission to first win the presidency and resolved to fulfill his campaign promises if he did win. Candidates and political pundits were on fearful notice that he was serious. Those who sought protection from scrutiny under the guise of political correctness were skewered. When they tried to fight back, he'd pounce, and Main Street America loved Donald Trump even more. MAGA hats and shirts were flying off the shelves in the heartland.

Candidate Trump showed utter and complete contempt for the very politicians who mainstream America was rejecting. The years of their hapless representatives failing to stand against what appeared to be an Obama juggernaut cost them their moral authority to lead.

GOP and blue-collar voters had tired of politicians who'd had a chance to address America's big problems head-on. Now they were ready for a street fighter who none of the smart people gave a chance. A man who sometimes made us cringe because our ears had become accustomed to the soft talk of accommodation and political numbness.

The quiet folks of America, who had played by all the rules and were now sweating in the frog pot, wanted someone who not only didn't care about speaking the King's English or living the rules of high society but openly mocked what the professional finger shakers from the media, academia, Hollywood, and politicians of both parties thought.

Donald Trump was a man who hated what he saw America becoming and refused to cater to those who enabled it by simply lowering the temperature. He seemed to despise those who either willfully promoted it or were too weak to stop it. He was running for the highest office of the land, promising to turn the fire off and take away the matches from the perpetrators and the perpetuators.

Conservative and heartland voters wanted out of the boiling pot. After ballot victory after ballot victory for Republicans were followed by disappointment after disappointment, they wanted someone who could cut through the nonsense and begin fighting for America again. And that desire overshadowed how they felt about his past racial insensitivities or sexual vulgarities. They chose and elected Donald Trump to be president of the United States because they thought that this could be America's last chance to get fiscal sanity, individual liberty, personal responsibility, and economic freedom back on track.

CHAPTER TWO

Post-Christian America Unfolds

> Whatever we once were, we are no longer a Christian
> nation—at least not just...
>
> —BARACK OBAMA, 2006

ABERCROMBIE & FITCH, a clothing store that brands
for its customers "a classic east coast collegiate style," had to
go to court because it used to prohibit its employees from wearing
hats and black clothing to work per its employee manual. In case you
are not familiar with the brand, it has stores in many malls with the
heavy cologne smell and loud music piercing from its doors to lure
customers inside.

In 2015, the U.S. Supreme Court ruled that the retailer wrongfully
did not hire a Muslim woman who came to her interview wearing a
head scarf, concluding that the dress policy of Abercrombie & Fitch
unfairly discriminated against her.[2]

It was not a close vote, decided by an 8–1 margin arguing, "Religious practice is one of the protected characteristics that cannot be
accorded disparate treatment and must be accommodated." Never
mind that one might wonder why a devout Muslim woman, religiously observant, would even want to work at Abercrombie & Fitch,

a business known for its edgy and sexualized apparel—or at a Hooters, Frederick's of Hollywood, Victoria's Secret, or gentlemen's club. But reasonable questions don't seem to matter when a bigger social agenda is on the table.

Still, this ruling and subsequent expansion of the legal meaning of discrimination changed the landscape for employers when it comes to accommodating their employees or even an applicant's religious beliefs. An almost-impossible guessing game for employers in post-Christian America, as declared by President Obama.

Yet the same Obama administration that pushed the Fitch case through the Equal Employment Opportunity Commission (EEOC) sued the Roman Catholic charity Little Sisters of the Poor to try to compel the nuns to include abortion in their Obamacare, government-mandated health insurance plans.[3]

In August 2011, the Department of Health and Human Services (HHS) issued a federal mandate that required employers to provide services like the week-after pregnancy interruption pill in their health insurance plans free of cost. The mandate did not exempt religious non-profits with religious objections, so a Catholic order of nuns that ran homes for the elderly poor across the country called the Little Sisters of the Poor fought back with help from the Becket law firm. After five years of court battles, in March 2016, the U.S. Supreme Court heard oral arguments in the case called *Zubik v. Burwell*, which was a consolidation of six cases brought by religious nonprofits against the federal Obamacare mandate, including the Little Sisters of the Poor.

In May 2016, the Supreme Court affirmed that the Little Sisters of the Poor did not have to provide abortion services as part of its plan. The Court did not do so based upon a religious faith test but instead due to the admission by the Obama administration that the government could provide those services using other means outside the health plan. On October 6, 2017, the Trump administration issued a new rule and admitted what it should have said all along: that the federal government violated the law when under the Obama administration it tried to force religious ministries like the Little Sisters to violate their faith.

What's important is that this case could have been easily settled without the Court at all given the facts. Yet for the Obama administration, it seemed to be more about power than the law, in that if the federal government could compel the Little Sisters of the Poor to pay for abortions through the health care law, it would have broken the back of Christian charitable groups by dictating what services they must provide to their employees using their private funds, thus destroying the moral DNA of Christian groups.

Somehow, in the Abercrombie & Fitch case, the Supreme Court ruled, with Judge Antonin Scalia writing the opinion, that company dress codes and uniforms be gone! A business needed to anticipate and accept accommodations for religious garb, facial hair, or other practices, and yet somehow the same Court couldn't find its way to provide a religious exemption to the Little Sisters of the Poor on abortion.

NOISY YET NECESSARY QUESTION

When can the voters of a state decide twice that they don't want a social policy to be changed and be overridden by a single federal court judge on the grounds that he didn't like the voters' decision?

In essence, that is exactly what happened in California in the seminal homosexual marriage case related to the legality of a state constitutional amendment known as Proposition 22.

In November 2008, in the same election in which Barack Obama won the presidency, more than 7 million California voters chose to oppose same-sex marriage at the ballot box, taking on the political left, Hollywood, Silicon Valley, and arguably the entire LGBTQ movement by voting in favor of Proposition 8. Proposition 8 was a ballot proposition to amend the state constitutional amendment to define marriage as between one man and one woman to address a California Supreme Court's May 2008 appeal ruling in the remarry

cases that followed the short-lived 2004 same-sex wedding contro-
versy.[4] Proponents of same-sex marriage garnered 6.4 million votes,
losing by a 52.2–47.8 margin with almost 80 percent of registered
voters turning out to the polls.

However, a judge appointed to the federal bench by President
George H. W. Bush overturned the wishes of the people of California, and his decision was upheld by a 2–1 margin at the appeals court
level, with the Supreme Court deciding to let the lower court's decision stand. The federal bench disenfranchised 7,001,084 Californians.

Later the judge who had made the initial ruling revealed that he
had been in a homosexual relationship for the preceding ten years,
but the Court subsequently ruled that his hidden history should not
be considered grounds for overturning his decision.

Proposition 8 was made necessary by an earlier 2008 California state court decision to invalidate a voter decision in 2000 that
declared that marriage was between a man and a woman. That initiative, known as Proposition 22, won by an overwhelming 61.4 to 38.6
percent in the 2000 election season.

The political class and the federal court in this case expanded the
culture war between the two conflicting worldviews competing for
the public square in America. These dominant forces that drive the
laws of our land had made it known clearly that they were no longer agents of the people, by and for the people, but were new moral
agents with the authority to drive a secular agenda.

Our nation was organized so that the states had certain degrees of
autonomy from the federal government to protect their sovereignty
against tyranny. In fact, the Tenth Amendment of our Constitution,
which is part of the Bill of Rights, specifically expresses the principle of federalism and states' rights, which strictly supports the entire
plan of the original Constitution for the United States of America
by stating that "the federal government possesses only those powers
delegated to it by the U.S. Constitution. All remaining powers are
reserved for the states or the people."

To the people of California, this protection in the Constitution

became meaningless, as the thuggery worldview o̷
could invalidate that voting mattered at all.

To drive the point home that those who don't agree̷
LWLP agenda need not apply in the Golden State, LGBTQ ac̷
scoured the records of those who dared to give money to support pa̷
sage of Proposition 8.

Soon the left discovered that the brilliant man Brendan Eich,
who invented JavaScript and was a co-founder and CEO of the Silicon Valley company Mozilla, had shown the audacity to make a
small donation of his own money to the Proposition 8 campaign.
The LWLP tolerance police descended on the company, and in short
order, Eich was out. Out—even though he took the same exact position as President Barack Obama on homosexual marriage during the
2008 general election.

ATTACKS ON CHRISTIAN PRINCIPLES IN THE PUBLIC SQUARE

In 2014, the high-tech executive and CEO of Mozilla was forced to
resign from the company he helped found and build because he made
a $1,000 contribution to support traditional marriage in the Califor-
nia marriage referendum. According to accounts, Brendan Eich was
subject to vicious attacks through social media for his contribution in
the marriage campaign.

Mozilla chairwoman Mitchell Baker observed, "Mozilla believes
in both equality and freedom of speech. Equality is necessary for
meaningful speech. And you need free speech to fight for equality.
Figuring out how to stand for both at the same time can be hard."
That Mozilla's chairwoman could offer such a confused, vacuous
explanation for Eich's dismissal sheds light on why discussions about
the overall state of affairs in our country is so noisy.

Free speech is not about a battle between equality and freedom.
Free speech includes the pursuit of truth. The equality necessary for
free speech is equality under the law, where everyone receives equal

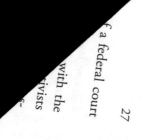

d not the truth—is our objective, ression gets flushed, and political ho lives and who dies.

on, a black Christian woman, began director of employee relations at the later became part of the University 2006. Shortly after the merger, Dixon ent for Human Resources-Health Science Camp , she was promoted to the position of interim associate vice president of Human Resources over all university campuses.

On April 3, 2008, Dixon read an opinion piece published in the *Toledo Free Press* that equated homosexual activities with the struggles of African American civil rights victims. Dixon disagreed with the viewpoint expressed in the column and decided to submit her own opinion piece to the *Toledo Free Press* to express her personal viewpoint on this matter of public concern. For this action, Crystal Dixon lost her job. According to the American Freedom Law Center, which handled Dixon's lawsuit, university officials knew Dixon's personal Christian views as far back as 2003, and they also knew that Dixon was impartial in her hiring and other employment-related practices "despite her personal biases," as was noted in Dixon's performance evaluations.[5]

Crystal Dixon was fired from her human resources position at the University of Toledo because she penned an op-ed during her personal time that challenged the proposition that the LGBTQ rights movement is a new chapter of the black civil rights movement. The university fought her lawsuit with venom and ceased providing her any benefits of employment. From the time she was fired in 2008 until 2011, Crystal Dixon had been unable to secure a comparable position with another employer and as a result has suffered and continues to suffer significant emotional and financial damage.

Carefully reasoned discourse—which is certainly what Dixon offered in her fatal op-ed—had become no longer welcomed in the politicized post-Christian society Obama had declared, making the

Trump phenomenon even more welcoming because pursuit of truth was no longer relevant and evangelical voters were getting nervous that they could be next in the unemployment line. They were noticing headline after headline that only behavior consistent with predetermined political ends would be welcome in the public square. This slippery slope was leading in one direction—to less freedom and more oppression with evangelical Christians in the hot seat. They needed someone to intervene, and in the opinion of many of their leaders, that someone was Donald Trump.

Stories of pursuit and persecution of devout Christians and other Americans who held traditional views on homosexuality were growing. A high-tech executive, the CEO of Twitter with an estimated net worth of $5 billion, was forced to offer a social media apology in June 2018 for eating a chicken sandwich at Chick-fil-A. Patronizing a fast-food establishment whose CEO is a devout Christian with the temerity to have criticized the Supreme Court decision legalizing same-sex marriage is a high crime in the eyes of far-left social media self-anointed as judges and juries. Russell Berger, chief knowledge officer of CrossFit, was fired for tweeting his support of a company decision to cancel participation of a CrossFit gym in Indianapolis in LGBTQ Pride Month events. Berger, a seminary-trained pastor, was perhaps excessively inflammatory because he used the word *sin*. If there is any "sin" in today's politicized America, it is to claim that sin, in the biblical sense, exists.

In the fall of 2017, I had to temporarily close my office in Washington because of threats when, in a cable TV interview, I equated the LGBTQ rainbow flag to the Confederate flag. From my point a view, it's a totally reasonable assertion. As an African American, the Confederate flag communicates to me that I am not welcome. As a Christian conservative American, the rainbow flag communicates to me that I am not welcome.

According to a recent Gallup survey, 41 percent of Americans identify as evangelical Christians. What this conservative public feared because of what has happened in America to traditional value can surely lend reason for why they supported Donald Trump.

THE IMPLODED RELIGIOUS RIGHT

Throughout our history, the traditional family model and Christianity reflected the presumed values for our country. And among all nations, America was seen as deeply religious, as remarked by de Tocqueville and other outsiders trying to discover the secret to our nation's success. From prohibition, to women's suffrage, to slavery, and to birth control, our laws were formed around Judeo-Christian convictions undergirded by founders who had confidence in the role of private churches, synagogues, and other religious orders in helping individuals self-govern.

As the seventies came upon an America that was limping out of the whirlwind of political and racial turmoil of the sixties, the debate around abortion raged in the media, pitting religion against freedom. When abortion become the law of the land in January 1973, America split in two: a culture war broke out over whether our country's public square would be governed by a dominant biblical society or by a dominant secular society.

LWLPs began to expand their secular worldview's influence over academia, entertainment, public policy, and the courts. Evangelicals and Catholics began to pull out of the public square by creating new private institutions to protect themselves and to teach their children the values that they believed brought prosperity to our nation. Many began to politically organize to remind Americans that the virtues that made America peaceful and prosperous were explicitly taught through our Judeo-Christian founding principles.

Three years after the legalization of abortion, Jimmy Carter, an evangelical from the South, won the nomination for the Democratic Party and became president of the United States.

While many in the religious right assumed that Carter held deep Christian convictions, others were disillusioned when he did not challenge the official position of the Democratic Party on abortion.

Sensing a loss of family values in our country without a president to defend them, the religious right began to organize under the leadership of Dr. Jerry Falwell, a Baptist pastor from Virginia. Bringing in Catholic, Jewish, and evangelical political action committees from across the country into one entity, Falwell created a movement called the Moral Majority to unify Christians to take action in politics.

As the Moral Majority worked through direct mail, rallies, television, and telephone, for decades our country had never seen a movement to change American public policy so organized, even forcing a debate on school prayer. Very little of the movement was geared toward the economic and racial disparities in the country, as the social issues, in particular legal abortion, were all-consuming politically.

The first major test of the strength of this new movement was its support for Ronald Reagan to become president, with Falwell endorsing him before the GOP convention.

Through the popularity of Ronald Reagan, the Moral Majority continued to operate through Reagan's second term, helping to bring him an electoral landslide in 1984 in which he won all states except for Minnesota.

President Reagan gained widespread popularity and historic results on international and economic concerns during his eight-year presidency, yet the country was still rapidly changing culturally. Throughout his tenure, the LWLPs, while still a bit invisible underground, were politically active and strategically vigilant in working to transform America into a totally secular state.

As the 1988 campaign season began, the religious right that had organized to expose and sabotage the left's agenda started to unravel. Televangelist Pat Robertson ran for president, creating divisions among some leaders in the Moral Majority. Dr. Jerry Falwell endorsed Vice President George Herbert Walker Bush in the primary against Pat Robertson. Dr. Bob Jones, whose Christian university was founded in 1927, challenged the Moral Majority's political positions.

Quickly, the Moral Majority dispersed, and its leaders went on to found other organizations, each with its own agenda and priorities, ending a unified national Christian political movement.

By 2015, forty years after the insurgence of the Moral Majority movement, abortion numbers had skyrocketed to 60 million, out-of-marriage births had grown to 40 percent, government expenditures had expanded to a fourth of the American economy, same-sex marriage had become the law of the land, and headlines were filled with Christian businesses being deluged by hate and government lawsuits demanding that they break with their deeply held biblical beliefs on marriage and abortion in order to not only accommodate but facilitate a secular worldview and society.

Whether it meant destroying the lives of Christian bakers because they declined to make wedding cakes for what the federal court has defined as homosexual marriage or of Iowa Mennonites who owned a wedding chapel but declined to allow same-sex marriages or of Christian florists, musicians, or any other service providers, the goal of the LWLPs had nothing to do with equal protection or homosexual marriage.

Instead it was to demonstrate that in an LWLP post-Christian America, the secular power of the state was supreme over God and over those who choose to follow Him.

In the new LWLP post-Christian America, it became right and just to hate biblical orthodoxy because despite differences in religious leaders of the right, average Bible believers weren't about to bow to any God but the one true God. And the one true God they believed in had outlined rules to live by, dos and don'ts that conflicted with secularism and with statism.

As quoted from my previous book, *Uncle Sam's Plantation*, according to theologian R. C. Sproul of Ligonier Ministries:

> Statism involves a philosophy of government by which the state, or government, is viewed not only as the final ruling authority but the ultimate agency of redemption.
>
> In this sense the state doesn't simply coexist with the church. It supplants the church. Statism can never function under God. If the state is deemed to be under God in the sense of being under God's authority and accountable to God for its actions, then the state cannot be the ultimate authority.[6]

In a post-Christian America, it also became right and just to hate capitalism and free markets because control is what matters to the progressive left, not equality of opportunity. It is the purpose of the new God-state to end disparate outcomes, no matter if those outcomes were based upon ability and work, faith, or family traditions.

Creator-God has an expectation of humanity to contribute according to one's individual uniqueness; God-state wants everyone to pretend that everyone should be exactly the same yet be able to make any kind of life choices they want without any consequences.

In an LWLP post-Christian America, it's right and just to hate our Constitution and our Declaration of Independence because the founders were rich white dudes, some of whom owned slaves.

The reality that all men are created equal, endowed by their Creator with certain unalienable rights, is recast to say that we were not created at all, that the Constitution is situational, and that each of us can make up our own reality.

Those who brought the Judeo-Christian ethos of moral absolutes, empowerment of capitalism, and embodiment of law into the Constitution to build the most advanced and free country in history must be brought down because, according to LWLP philosophy, these concepts are rooted in white privilege of a Western civilization that foisted biblical authority onto the world stage just to control minorities.

The LWLP social warriors who forced Brendan Eich to leave Mozilla, who put forward the full force of a new social construct to destroy Christian businesses and voices all across America, who even had the audacity to employ the full power of the federal government to try to force the Little Sisters of the Poor to their knees in front of their new power mandate all have something in common.

They spend every day trying to destroy the pillars upholding the Judeo-Christian nation that they were either raised in or moved to. Tolerance is something for everyone else to use, but they believe it is their moral right and obligation to be intolerant of Christianity and to mainstream their hatred.

Very few Americans were paying close attention to the battles raging in our culture war of the past fifty years. Not only were they unaware of the concentrated progressive agenda eating away at the founding fabrics of our institutions, they were unaware of the religious right trying to fight that agenda. What they concluded about political news was it was noisy, so they tuned out. Most people other than the activists, the political pundits, and the Beltway lawyers, legislators, and lobbyists were unaware that an America-loathing cancer was growing from within, let alone that it had metastasized. But during the Obama years, the heartland started to really feel the pain.

Large numbers of evangelicals began hitting the airwaves and social media to voice their discontent that leadership of the religious right had become impotent in its ability to uphold moral authority against the collapse of our culture. Their discontent compelled them to become part of a Tea Party groundswell that began rumbling in 2009 to sound an alarm of the big battle raging for the soul of America. Donald Trump's rise was proof that enough evangelicals knew deep in their hearts that continuing down a path of disdain for Christianity didn't offer any real solutions to the most pressing problems of the country.

CHAPTER THREE

Rise of the Tea Party and Donald Trump

I N 1994, amid a void of cohesive political leadership from the religious right, Republicans came roaring back into congressional power under the leadership of Newt Gingrich and Dick Armey with the Contract with America. The contract made ten promises to the American people, and all but one was signed into law.

The contract was an olive branch to Republican loyalists to show them the GOP had heard their cry for effective leadership to reduce taxes, to reduce the size and scope of government, and to balance the federal budget—things President H. W. Bush had said he would do but hadn't, and as a result, in 1992, a Democratic governor from Arkansas had become president with a Democratic Congress.

Then the American voters took a chance with the promise of the contract and turned congressional power over to the GOP. On November 8, 1994, the U.S. House of Representatives election known as the Republican Revolution was held in the middle of President Bill Clinton's first term.

As a result of a fifty-four-seat swing in membership from Democrats to Republicans, the Republican Party gained a majority of seats in the House for the first time since 1952 and a majority of votes for the first time since 1946.

It was the largest seat gain for the Republican Party since 1946 and the largest for either party since 1948. The Democrats had run the House for all but four of the preceding sixty-two years.

I cannot forget this moment in history as I not only worked in the heartland to promote the Contract with America, but after the red team won, I worked tirelessly with them to get welfare reform passed and signed into law. As a result, I was honored to speak at the GOP National Convention in 1996 and was the one selected to check the box upon the completion of Welfare Reform, promise number 8.

The only promise of the contract that didn't become law was number ten: term limits. The Potomac swamp had become comfortable for many of the signers of the contract, so there was little political will around passing number ten. Many of the conservative good guys holding up their term limit promise to their constituents termed themselves out, and the GOP swelled into a political comfort zone in their absence.

William Jefferson Clinton left office with an increasingly divided and culturally collapsed country. George Walker Bush left office with an even more divided and culturally collapsed country.

Republicans were unceremoniously dumped from their twelve-year hold on congressional power as the promise of the Contract with America descended into a cloud of lobbyist scandals, the Iraq War, and idea fatigue. The GOP Congress forgot that they were elected as reformers. They forgot that they were not elected to pretend the Potomac was perfume when it was actually a poison slowly killing our country.

The late, great Robert Novak wrote of this "Republican blindness" in his November 9, 2006, post-election *Washington Post* column titled such. "Even up to the last minute, the Republicans never really saw overall defeat coming," he opined. "Republican Senator Lindsey Graham of South Carolina used a golfer's language in telling me last July that his colleagues failed to appreciate how close the Republicans were to losing control of the Senate: 'It's like we think we'll get by with pars on the last two holes when we really need birdies,' he said then. On Wednesday Graham told me: 'Actually, we bogeyed the 17th hole and picked up on the 18th.' "

Senator Graham was right. After twelve years in power, the congressional GOP leadership was out of steam with a sitting president who was in his fifth year of war and not faring particularly well. Anti-GOP protests were fed by a mass media machine and the good news of the economy was derided as only creating burger-flipper jobs, while the manufacturing sector continued to be hollowed out by the full effects of NAFTA and Red China being granted permanent normalized trade relations.

The fragmented national leadership of the religious right was unprepared to speak to these heartland concerns. While many religious coalitions worked on campaigns and legislation on the local level, there was no national religious right organized to push beyond social issues.

The few religious right groups inside the Beltway didn't notice that their constituencies of Christian voters were growing weary as they saw little movement on ending abortion or on holding back the LWLPs aggressive attack within academia and entertainment and on their families. Even the donors of evangelical policy groups were tiring of the financial hit as government grew and their religious leaders remained silent on the economy.

Predictably, voters who had historically been loyal supporters of the GOP majority went missing in action. Their so-called elected reformers had become pork-happy in the swamp of tax and spend. Voters could rarely tell the difference between electing Democrats and Republicans, so in 2006 a majority of voters gave America a full taste of what Democratic control of Congress was like with Speaker Nancy Pelosi in the House and Majority Leader Harry Reid in the Senate. Two years later, in 2008, Barack Obama would be elected to become the forty-fourth president of the United States of America.

With this backdrop, a Tea Party revolution began to organize as a movement in 2009 that had little to do with wanting to return Republicans to power but everything to do with taking the phone and pen from Obama and the gavel and power from House Speaker Nancy Pelosi.

The first sign of a Tea Party groundswell taking hold nationally was the political earthquake that shook the polls after Alaska Governor Sarah Palin accepted the GOP nomination for vice president with the type of call-to-arms speech that Republican, Independent, and what remained of conservative Democrat voters had not heard since President Ronald Reagan left the stage. A staggering McCain campaign suddenly jumped into the lead in the polls throughout early September 2008 as people were excited by the young dynamism of the charismatic governor willing to take on presidential candidate Obama with zeal.

But wind was already behind the sails of the Democrats. They had nominated an incredible orator whose energy alone made the presidential campaign of John McCain look frail and fractured. Even the newfound enthusiasm that Governor Palin brought to the ticket began to wane immediately after the incredibly poor decision to put her into a series of taped interviews with the seasoned and savvy media guru Katie Couric that, once edited, made Palin look unprepared for the job.

Unlike David, who had refused to wear battle armor when he entered the national stage against Goliath, Palin's national media faux pas compounded early decisions on wardrobe choices and their costs with late-night comics mocking her every move and word. Conservative and heartland American voters were unaccustomed to these types of vicious and relentless personal attacks against a political candidate for the vice presidency, in particular against a well-qualified and charismatic female leader. And they were enraged by them.

When presidential candidate John McCain then made what many grassroots Republican voters considered two major catastrophic decisions—one, to give back endorsements from two very prominent and influential evangelical leaders, pastors John Hagee and Rod

Parsley; and second, to stop his campaign and go back to Washington to deal with the financial crisis by embracing the big bank bailouts—the election was over. Barack Obama was elected in an overwhelming victory, and the Democrats' hold on Congress continued.

But the heartland of America was awakened by Sarah Palin because they saw in her a fire to fight. They didn't want to drown in the frog pot. They were getting desperate for a leader who would fight for them. They saw themselves in her as she forcefully endorsed her love of God and guns. Her patriotism was electrifying. To fill the void of GOP leadership, remnants of Congressman Ron Paul's campaign rallied behind Sarah Palin as a figurehead, and a new brand of libertarian populism began to rise, similar to the momentum that grew behind Newt Gingrich's Contract with America.

Many political observers agree that the twenty-first-century Tea Party movement began in January 2009 after newly elected President Barack Obama announced administrative plans to give financial aid to bankrupt homeowners. Following a February 2009 call by CNBC reporter Rick Santelli on the floor of the Chicago Mercantile Exchange for a "Chicago tea party," more than fifty center/right activists agreed by conference call to coalesce against Obama's agenda and thus scheduled a series of protests that culminated in the 2009 Taxpayer March on Washington.

The Tea Party was now a well-organized force and it began to immediately fight the growth of government with full steam and with the repeal of Obamacare as its focus. Its new battle-cry banner of limited government flew high with a groundswell of both enthusiasm and anger. With AWOL national Christian leadership, the interests of social issues took a back seat.

Disillusionment and disgust with congressional Republican leadership were real within the Tea Party as the memories of the seemingly steady stream of lobbyist scandals made the people wary of the GOP brand, but it seized an opportunity to take over the GOP with liberty lovers in the primaries. It even recruited me! In 2007, I had moved my CURE headquarters from Los Angeles to Washington,

D.C., so the decision couldn't be made lightly. But I didn't want to wake up the day after the 2010 election and ask myself why I didn't at least try. With an endorsement from Sarah Palin and other liberty-loving leaders, I took a five-month hiatus from CURE, left my home in Orange County, California, and moved into the Los Angeles district that included the cities of Compton and Carson and half the city of Long Beach to run for Congress against an incumbent LWLP Congressional Black Caucus member. All across America liberty lovers were leaving their businesses, jobs, pulpits, and homemaking to run for political office. And I wasn't the only black conservative inspired to run in 2010 due to the energy of the Tea Party. Fourteen others ran in their respective states as the Buffalo Soldiers within the newly formed groundswell.

But most in the Washington, D.C., establishment class could not see the political tsunami heading in their direction. While one of D.C.'s best GOP consultants, Tony Marsh, was arguing in a Townhall.com piece that the Republicans could win back the House by offering a "contrasting and visionary message to America," the highly respected Stu Rothenberg expressed the view of the vast major-ity of the political chattering class when he dismissed Marsh and wrote in his April 2010 Rothenberg Political Report, "Yes, Repub-licans have plenty of opportunities in good districts following their loss of 53 House seats over the past two cycles. And yes, there are signs that the Republican hemorrhage has stopped and even possibly that the party's fortunes have begun to reverse course..." Rothenberg adamantly declared, "But there are no signs of a dramatic rebound for the party, and the chance of Republicans winning control of either chamber in the 2010 midterm elections is zero. Not 'close to zero.' Not 'slight' or 'small.' Zero...Big changes in the House require a political wave," he overconfidently said like a good elite liberal. "You can cherry-pick your way to a five- or eight-seat gain, but to win doz-ens of seats, a party needs a wave."

Oops.

Six months later, in September 2010, before the wave that brought

Republicans back to power was fully apparent, Democratic pollster Doug Schoen and GOP pollster Scott Rasmussen published the prescient book *Mad as Hell: How the Tea Party Movement Is Effectively Remaking Our Two-Party System*, which in the rearview mirror of time was genius. Rasmussen in an interview on the book told Newsmax, "Tea Party participants think federal spending, deficits and taxes are too high, and they think no one in Washington is listening to them, and that latter point is really, really important." The back jacket of the book describes the movement as follows: "The Tea Party movement is not a flash in the pan, as many have assumed. Nor is it a movement of racist rednecks and ignorant boobs, as its detractors have crudely suggested. To the contrary, it is an authentic grassroots movement of concerned American citizens demanding to be heard by an out-of-touch political establishment. Their concerns are real and their issues are legitimate..."

The failure of GOP swamp bathers to provide the Tea Party leadership anything but disdain gave rise to Donald Trump for the presidency of the United States.

ENTER DONALD TRUMP

Yes, the same Donald Trump who ran for president in 2000 against George W. Bush as the Reform Party candidate and political Independent. His candidacy at that time got very little attention because he withdrew from the race in February 2000, four months after announcing his bid. According to press reports, Trump cited infighting in the Reform Party as not "conducive to victory," concluding that he could not win the general election as the party's nominee. He had expressed concerns about the direction of the party, particularly its membership, referring to David Duke, Pat Buchanan, and Lenora Fulani as a Klansman, a neo-Nazi, and a Communist, respectively. Donald Trump took his 2000 defeat seriously and studiously. He retooled his position and announced his 2016 candidacy as a Republican with strong backing of the Tea Party grass roots. His focused primary target was the GOP political establishment and Governor Jeb Bush, who was front and center.

Other candidates such as former Arkansas Governor Mike Huckabee, a leader within the religious right movement, and Senator Ted Cruz, a leader within the Tea Party movement, tried to position themselves away from the Bush/Trump contention and attempted to rally Christian conservatives. But without a national movement behind either, Christian conservatives had become just as concerned with economic issues as they once were with social issues and began to attend Trump rallies. Notably, the son of the late Moral Majority founder Jerry Falwell endorsed Trump early in his candidacy, and in February 2016 Christian Coalition founder Pat Robertson said, "Trump inspires us all."

One thing you don't hear from the media on either the right or the left is that Donald Trump is smart—shrewdly smart. But it is true. The GOP establishment, the left-wing media, and even the pundits who supported him never mentioned this simple fact—Donald Trump is both inherently witty and clever, even as he lets everyone in his circles play a role. It is not an accident that he controls the daily narrative for the entire news world through his Twitter account. While the establishment media, the LWLPs, and his political opponents in Swampland called Trump a bully, this may be the only thing about him that they got right. What they miss about Trump is that being a bully is why he is the president.

I don't watch many movies, probably have only seen ten in my lifetime. But friends tell me about movies all the time, and on this topic one friend, who is a big supporter of Trump, told me about a movie he saw in the eighties called *My Bodyguard*. It was about a kid who was tired of being pushed around so he hired the biggest kid in school to act as his protector against the self-designated kings of the school. My friend said the reason he supported Trump from the beginning was "that the political establishment had become the mean girl, hard guy archetype who made it unsafe for anyone not in their clique to go into certain bathrooms for fear of getting pounded. Donald Trump was the exact tough guy that much of America was looking for to remind the D.C. know-it-alls who they work for." Didn't see the movie, but, okay, I get the point.

Sarah Palin had shown that the undercurrent for a real political wave existed. The Tea Party had shown that the wave could be a dynamic force in politics even when there wasn't a real leader at the helm. And now Donald Trump had captured that momentum and expanded it by speaking for Americans who loved their country but wondered why their country did not love them back. The forgotten Americans, many of whom served in the military, came home and discovered that their towns were closing down due to the Republican-encouraged export of their jobs and a Democrat war on Americans who worked growing crops, extracting wealth from the ground, and building things. These Americans found in Donald Trump a bully who was on their side.

Every election these forgotten Americans, who cling to God and their guns found themselves having to choose between a candidate who supported the Second Amendment and espoused their cultural values—but who also did not seem to care about their ability to have a great job that paid enough for them to take care of their families; and a candidate who wanted their tax dollars to pay for abortions and would take their guns in a heartbeat—but who would talk a populist economic game bemoaning the loss of jobs without a prescription to save them.

It was time for action. The patience of white, heterosexual, blue-collar, male voters had worn thin. And tapping their feet or wringing their hands or biting their tongues was no longer an option. The year 2016 was time to make America great again. And with that, Donald Trump became the voice for voters who the political elites in both political parties had stopped listening to. Donald Trump was the people's bully. A people who knew that neither CEOs nor presidents have to hold PhDs on every subject to be great leaders. What the media claimed as a failure of intellect they saw as actually the superior one because processing information is all a computer or a brain does. Some of the noise in the White House, in the Cabinets, and on K Street upon Trump's arrival as president was about him not patting the ego of anyone, much less the Beltway swamp dwellers who have spent lifetimes inside the Beltway establishment. Much of the turnover in his administration represents folks who were shown the door less than fifteen minutes into a briefing with a president with a businessman's brain. Much of the leaking was the bruised ego of the expert.

The goal of governance is not to make smart technocrats feel good but is instead to come to the right decisions based upon both the facts and the point of view of the elected president. Just a month into his presidency, it should have been obvious to any open-minded observers that Donald Trump is very, very good at listening, asking, and deciding—after all, unlike most politicians who spend a lifetime avoiding accountability while clamoring for more power, Trump has only known the harshness of eating his mistakes and enjoying the rewards of successes. Some call this a lack of curiosity; business guru and author Michael Maccoby identified these types of widely misunderstood personality types as "productive narcissists" in his 2003 book of the same title. It really is nothing more than cutting to the chase. If you trust the briefer, you know you can get all the details that went into the decision without reading them and studying them yourself. You hear the alternative, you ask questions, you make a decision, and you move to the next item on your plate.

Trump is a leader. And his leadership style is one dependent on trust and loyalty from absolutely everyone near him and working with and for him. All one had to do was go to an event where he was speaking in the early Iowa caucus season to see that people naturally gravitated to Donald Trump, who has an innate charisma. Some of what drew people was the celebrity factor, and some of it was curiosity, but most of it was the trust and loyalty of his followers because they saw him as genuine and honest. Donald Trump seems to get his energy from trust and loyalty because he is genuine and honest— oftentimes brutally honest. Yes, it is true that when Donald Trump entered a room, an almost electric charge coursed through the crowd.

The sooner the GOP embraces his leadership, the sooner Republicans can get about addressing the hard problems in our country. Once the decision is made to trust and be loyal to the instincts of our duly elected President Donald Trump, the GOP could actually get some credit as he fulfills the promises of his inauguration. And once the decision is made to respect the insights of the folks in the heartland as our president's promises take hold, the GOP may actually expand its base in 2020.

PART TWO

TOLERANCE
NOISE

CHAPTER FOUR

Immigration Madness

From this day forward, a new vision will govern our land. From this moment on, it's going to be America First. Every decision on trade, on taxes, on immigration, on foreign affairs, will be made to benefit American workers and American families. We must protect our borders from the ravages of other countries making our products, stealing our companies, and destroying our jobs. Protection will lead to great prosperity and strength.

—DONALD TRUMP, 2017 inaugural address

H E TOLD US that he was shutting the border. He told border jumpers not to bring their kids. He told the world that he had no tolerance for the drugs, gangs, and illegal cheap labor pouring into America. But the LWLPs were so determined to maintain their political status quo that they used desperate migrants fleeing corrupted countries and their conspiring media to capture photos.

Oops. Pushed the wrong person.

President Trump understands his supporters, and Trump supporters get it. They know that slavery was wrong and that segregation was a national sin. Most Americans today have a mix of many ethnicities in their workplaces, friendships, and families. But with major cities and states creating sanctuary spaces for illegal immigrants, many believe the multicultural tolerance thing has gone way too far.

I remember the story one of my dear friends conveyed as she was working her way up to principal in a major school district in California. She had to become fluent in Spanish for the next tier in her career because the schools were enrolling record numbers of non-English-speaking students. She went through an intense summer immersion course in Mexico only to find years later after becoming a principal that the school district hierarchy preferred that she not graduate students so quickly from her third-grade English as a second language (ESL) courses because the district was losing money assigned per student in these ESL classes.

Our national debate on immigration policy centers on a paradox that we must be aware of to deal with this issue properly. The United States needs an immigration policy because a lot of people want to come here. If that weren't the case, we wouldn't need an immigration policy. But because LWLP lobby groups on immigration policy like the National Council of La Raza and the ACLU oppose assimilation and English-only instruction in schools, new immigrants use their native language in America, making translators and multilinguists needed in almost every public- and private-sector industry.

Why do people want to come? For freedom. Because where there is freedom, there is opportunity. But freedom conflicts with the worldview of multiculturalism. And over the past sixty years of our nation's culture war, multiculturalism has spiraled into immigration madness.

The immigration issue has become a political football within this culture war because of the political baggage it carries.

Both major political parties want votes from the Hispanic population as Hispanics are the most rapidly growing demographic in the country. And yet this is the same population most sensitive to the immigration issue because most of the illegals within our borders are from Latin American countries.

And herein lies the paradox. The purported strategy to attract Hispanic votes is not about engaging this population to preserve American culture, freedom, and opportunity, which is what make the United States so attractive to those who want to come.

The strategies are about how to pander to this population. Those in the heartland who are all in for American culture—not encouraging this segment of our population toward assimilation, embracing the English language, or accepting capitalism and our Constitution—had grown tired by the time of the 2016 election.

In poll after poll, majorities of Hispanics embrace the view that government has a positive role in creating more opportunities for citizens who were not born to privilege. But the problem is that most whites in America view their lives not as privileged but simply ones of hard work.

America was built by hundreds of millions of legal immigrants coming here to be free. Yet we are now told by the LWLPs that the immigrants of today must be offered special government concessions and considerations because they are minority groups of color, including those who enter illegally. Let's recall that even the demographic category "Hispanic" is a purely political construction, devoid of any racial or ethnic reality, designed only for special interest lobbying.

Historian Paul Johnson, in his *History of the American People*, relates how this category was created in the 1960s through the lobbying efforts of "the Mexican-American Legal Defense and Education Fund, a powerful interest group in alliance with the Democratic Party…" Today, immigrants from more than twenty countries are considered "Hispanic," while some Americans of European ancestry are asking what exactly people from Mexico, Puerto Rico, Spain, Cuba, Guatemala, and Argentina have in common that has afforded them the privilege to build a wedge of hostility between themselves and traditional American culture. It is in the history of America that immigrants have come from around the world for the opportunity of living free. All share a history of struggle, of facing discrimination because they are different but overcoming it all to become Americans.

Through their histories, Native Americans and African Americans are unique in their station in America. But Hispanic immigrants are no different from other immigrants who came to America by choice seeking opportunity and freedom. For since the founding of America there has been a steady stream of millions who want to migrate to the United States to be adopted into her beautiful culture and land of the free. But the dogma that has been promoted by the left through multiculturalism has blurred the lines of responsibility for the new migrants. The left has insisted on a welfare system that includes anyone who applies legally or not, working or not, trying or not, so more are migrating by any means necessary. And the left has promoted ideas of identity politics that have segregated folks based on their ethnicity, so more are not mainstreaming.

LOST IN MULTICULTURAL DEMAGOGUERY

In 2018, when Alexandria Ocasio-Cortez rocketed into the national spotlight as a result of her stunning primary victory over incumbent Democrat Joe Crowley in New York's 14th congressional district to take that seat in the House of Representatives, media and political pundits wondered aloud how this young woman who had never held or run for political office could beat a ten-term incumbent by fifteen points when his funds were by some estimates fifteen times greater than hers. They also pointed out that she is a declared socialist, wants government health care for all, wants all college tuitions paid for with federal taxes, is an outspoken advocate for the LGBTQ agenda, and is an aggressive critic of Israel.

According to the Census Bureau, NY 14 breaks down demographically as 22 percent white, 50 percent Hispanic, 9 percent black, and 16 percent Asian. In addition, 45.8 percent in this district are foreign born, and 67.8 percent report that they speak a language other than English at home. In political terms, NY 14 is defined as a majority-minority district. Districts like these had intensified discussions on immigration policy leading up to the election of Donald Trump.

Consider Puerto Rico, where Ms. Ocasio-Cortez traces her roots, which is an economic basket case as a result of the same kind of big government ideas that Ocasio-Cortez is telling the constituents of NY 14 they need for a better life. According to scholar Desmond Lachman of the American Enterprise Institute, "Over the past decade, the Puerto Rican economy has shrunk 10 percent while more than 10 percent of its population has migrated to the mainland. At the same time its unemployment rate remains over 12 percent and barely 40 percent of its population participates in the labor market."

Hurricane Maria in 2017 shone a spotlight on the fact that Puerto Rico's public finances were seriously compromised in large measure due to years of economic mismanagement, which led to a large public deficit, an excessive public debt-to-GDP ratio, a very large amount of unfunded pension liabilities, and thus Puerto Rico's inability to bounce back from the severe storm. While Ms. Ocasio-Cortez came to Washington promising everyone a free lunch paid for by the U.S. government, the Congressional Budget Office was issuing warnings of the same problems in our nation—huge deficits and crushing national debt—that had crippled Puerto Rico.

Although NY 14 is very different from the average American congressional district, the demographic changes of our nation are headed in that direction. Per the Census Bureau, more than 50 percent of Americans today age five and below are not white. But LWLP demagogues like Alexandria Ocasio-Cortez try to blind ethnic minorities with distortions that somehow big government socialism, the softer side of communism, will work in America. Trump supporters are demanding that the demagoguery stops and that those who want to destroy Americanism are stopped from coming in the first place.

NATIONAL BORDERS INTOLERANCE

Running a country is an art, not a science. If it were science, we could write software and send everybody in Washington home. Leadership is art, and while the late John Lennon said in his 1970s epic classic

Imagine that he may be a "dreamer" for imagining a world where there were no countries, he was an entertainment artist. Donald Trump, on the other hand, is an entrepreneurial artist who understands what our country is about and is willing to make the tough calls when things are not black and white.

And there are many difficult decisions to be made—beyond the smoke and mirrors of dreaming—to answer tough questions about communism and multiculturalism.

The questions of how many foreign-born people should be allowed to legally immigrate into the United States, what standards the U.S. government should use to determine who should be given visas, and the rules on how foreign-born legal U.S. residents can move toward citizenship have all been set aside as a more fundamental question has taken over the immigration debate: Does the United States have the right to deport those who have entered the country illegally?

What happens when hundreds of thousands flood any country's borders illegally, even those claiming amnesty, and overrun that country's systems and culture? Does a country have the right to refuse them and deport those who got around the laws of legal entry?

How about the visa overstay problem we also have in America?

In 2017, the Department of Homeland Security reported that it believes that 1.25 percent of the more than 50 million people issued temporary visas to come to the United States that year were suspected of overstaying their visa. What do you do with someone who went to school in the United States and now wishes to put their talents to work for a U.S. company? Some sources estimate that 40 percent of folks in America illegally work for a U.S. company.

So, yes, the immigration debate is noisy. But brace yourself because this is a necessary debate as much of the noise you hear today driving immigration policy is rooted in the John Lennon philosophical question of whether borders should exist at all.

Liberal opponents of borders point to income disparity between nations and the inherent unfairness that someone born into a very poor country is significantly disadvantaged compared with someone born into a very wealthy country.

Libertarian border opponents, on the other hand, essentially argue that borders are artificial barriers impeding the right for an individual to move to wherever he or she wants so long as no harm is done to others.

And, of course, the economic argument that a free flow of labor is good for businesses as it provides a cushion against labor shortages with the resulting lowering of labor costs is a constant rationale for either ending or at least dramatically opening borders.

President Donald Trump succinctly stated the case for borders when he said, "A nation without borders is not a nation." The immigration debate is about law, and law is about defining lines you don't cross, whether it is the physical lines that define the borders of our nation or the legal lines that protect the life, liberty, and property of citizens. Those who came here illegally of their own volition have violated both, and this cannot be tolerated. President Trump is making every effort to keep his promise to fix our nation's immigration policy, which includes securing our borders. And although headlines of children being separated from adults crossing our borders illegally are uncomfortable, it is for the sake of our freedom that we must bear the discomfort.

In short, while the ideals of freedom that each of us is "endowed by their Creator with certain unalienable rights" clearly extend to all of humanity, the operating document that created the government of the United States set up laws and prohibitions on government encroachments on these individual liberties. Some libertarians forget the basic truth that should borders cease to exist, the Constitution itself and those guarantees of individual rights lose their jurisdiction, becoming little more than the very old paper they were written on. Unfettered immigration does not allow a government the ability to even meet its own national security needs to protect against those who mean to do harm to the people of the United States and to its duly elected government. A government's very legitimacy comes immediately into question as strategically located foreign, illegal voters could do more to disrupt the election process than all the purported Russian Facebook ads combined.

In 2000, President George W. Bush defeated Vice President Al Gore in the state of Florida by a mere 547 votes, tipping the electoral college to Bush. In the 2016 Trump election, the president won Michigan, Pennsylvania, and Wisconsin by fewer than 80,000 votes total. A more strategic wielding of illegal alien vote casting using anonymous mail-in voter registrations and ballots in these three states, and Hillary Clinton would have been elected.

In addition to voter integrity concerns with illegals obtaining drivers licenses and being counted in the census, illegal immigration puts extra burdens on our taxpayer-funded assistance programs and private charities. The already-overwhelmed social structure for aid that we have established for our nation's poor will completely break down as more and more of the poorest in the world come to America and discover they can be wealthier than they ever imagined without ever getting an on-the-books job.

John Lennon wrote and sung the words to *Imagine* more than forty years ago. He should have known better based upon his own four-year legal battle to stay in the United States after his visa extension was denied. You see, John could see his idyllic view of a world without borders, but when it came to his own life, he desperately wanted to remain in the United States. Imagine that.

THE GREAT SEAL OF THE UNITED STATES

Lodged in the beak of the eagle at the center of the Great Seal of the United States is a banner with the words *E pluribus unum*: "Out of many, one." The U.S. State Department provides a fascinating history of the development of the Great Seal, which took six years to complete, from the time that Congress directed that it be developed in 1776 to the time it was approved in 1782. If there is one theme that emerges from the many symbols engraved in our national seal, it is the unification of diversity into singularity. Or, to see it from the opposite perspective, the penetration of a single unifying truth, uniting its diverse components.

If you look closely at the Great Seal, you will see the preponderance of the number thirteen: the thirteen founding colonies and their unification into a new nation, thirteen stars arranged into a single pattern of the Star of David, and the Eagle holding thirteen arrows in one of its talons and in the other an olive branch with thirteen leaves. So, in addition to the unification of the thirteen colonies, our national seal shows the unification of the opposites of war and peace—both key and opposing elements in an overall and unifying truth. Upon studying the Great Seal, you can't miss the fact that it conveys the sense of biblical truth that the founders of the nation had regarding the mission they were on and the great project they had undertaken.

Our current debate about immigration, legal and illegal, is being held hostage by the worldview of those who hate the principles of our founding. The embrace of biblical truth was succinctly expressed in the establishment of our nation. Congress passed a resolution in 1956, and President Eisenhower signed into law that the official motto of the United States would be "In God We Trust." And God has guidelines. Rules. Laws. Including guidelines, rules, and laws regarding immigration. *E pluribus* without God is chaos and rule by politicians. American culture has come under attack under the guise of tolerance, and this attack has many fronts. New migrants, illegal immigrants, and the foreign-born children of illegal immigrants are simply a means to an end to be politically manipulated for the political agenda of the left.

It is the intention of progressives to exchange the concept of *E pluribus unum* for multiculturalism, and multiculturalism means big government, collectivism, and control. Sort of like communism? Yep. Just like communism. Progressives want to pretend that there is no defined American culture, and they call anyone who says there is racist, homophobic, sexist, and white privileged. Yet our Constitution was about doing the job of uniting the separate states with their diverse interests into one nation defined by unifying, eternal principles. Its objective was one nation with national protections "to secure the blessings of liberty for ourselves and our posterity." Yet what is a blessing if not what is good in the eyes of God?

CHAPTER FIVE

Cappie or Commie

In a higher phase of communist society, after the enslaving
subordination of the individual to the division of labor,
and therewith also the antithesis between mental and physical labor, has vanished; after labor has become not only
a means of life but life's prime want; after the productive
forces have also increased with the all-around development
of the individual, and all the springs of co-operative wealth
flow more abundantly—only then can the narrow horizon
of bourgeois right be crossed in its entirety and society
inscribe on its banners: From each according to his ability,
to each according to his need.

—KARL MARX

THE MERRIAM-WEBSTER Dictionary definition of capitalism is "an economic system characterized by private or corporate ownership of capital goods, by investments that are determined
by private decision, and by prices, production and the distribution of
goods that are determined mainly by competition in a free market."
Socialism, in contrast, is defined as "any of various economic and
political theories advocating collective or governmental ownership and

administration of the means of production and distribution of goods."
Communism is the political theory derived from Karl Marx, advocating class war and leading to a society in which all property is publicly
owned and each person works and is paid according to their abilities
and needs, which is similar to socialism except that while socialism is
political force by persuasion, communism is political force by the gun.

The battle between individual choice and self-determination and
the purported collective good is at the center of America's economic
and, indeed, political debate. Because if each individual does not
control the products of their own labors or conceived by their own
minds, then they are little more than a slave to those who determine
the collective good.

In 1913, the U.S. Constitution was amended to allow the imposi-
tion of an income tax. The first fundamental decision was that the tax
would be progressive, meaning that those who earned more income
would pay a higher percentage of that income to the federal government. And with that decision, the key philosophy of communism
took root: that Americans should be treated unequally by the government based upon their wealth. This philosophy was encoded into
the DNA of the United States, and our system of capitalism has been
under attack since.

The original top tax rate was 7 percent, with the lowest earners
paying 1 percent. Within five years, the top rate had been increased
to 77 percent, as the still-nascent Federal Reserve hadn't yet discovered the magic of massive borrowing to shelter voters from the consequences of their decisions and the European war that Democratic
President Woodrow Wilson had campaigned against entering in 1916
needed to be paid for.

The very wealthy, who earned $1 million or more, only got to
keep twenty-three cents out of every dollar they made over a million.
But don't fret: they got to keep twenty-four cents of every dollar they
made above $500,000 up to a million and a whopping silver quarter
of each dollar made between $300,000 and $499,000.

Income earned by the people of the United States effectively became the property of the government, with the only question being how much the government would allow one to have.

This philosophy of communism continues in America's tax code today because the Democratic party is deeply invested in it. In the 2016 tax cut/reform debate, Democratic Representative Nancy Pelosi of San Francisco, California, argued that the tax bill was a "disgusting smash and grab" and "an all-out looting of America, a wholesale robbery of the middle class." She went on to say, "The GOP tax scam will go down, again, as one of the worst, most scandalous acts of plutocracy in our history."

And what was the tax bill's crime that unglued Ms. Pelosi? The tax bill President Trump signed into law in December 2017 lowered taxes for a vast majority of Americans. It also lowered the corporate tax rate from the highest in the industrialized world to one of the lowest 25 percent in the world. It offered parents tax-free opportunities to save more money for their children's education, and it opened opportunity for capital gains savings on monies invested in our country's most distressed zip codes.

What most missed in the tax debate was that neither Republicans nor Democrats argued against Marx's basic premise for a progressive tax system. "From each according to his ability, to each according to his need" is the economic philosophy most killing our economic system, and seldom, if ever, in the fervor of tax reform was heard a simple defense of the concept that used to rally Republican voters in the Reagan era—for an end to the progressive system and the institution of the flat tax—where every American paid the same percentage rate with no deductions regardless of their income level. Or a consumption tax where everyone pays at the pump, so to speak.

In essence, hyperbole aside, leaders of both political parties accepted the underlying premise that government should redistribute wealth, and the only question was how much the government should allow the people to keep.

Given the intellectual collapse of Republican legislators who were entrusted by voters to defend capitalism, is there any question why those who seek to completely annihilate the liberties associated with owning the product of one's own labor, intellectual creation, or investment have been emboldened to come out from the shadows and honestly demand forcible redistribution, also known as communism?

Hence, the meteoric rise of the Antifa and Indivisible movements.

The debate over America's tax system is still alive in the hearts of those who believed in capitalism under President Reagan and who will probably energetically rally to reelect Donald Trump to get this tax debate settled once and for all. Will America's tax system be rooted in capitalism or communism?

The few and faithful defenders of capitalism left in our country know they will need a leader with the resolve of Ronald Reagan to get this question answered; thus, I'm certain they will remind Trump during his reelection campaign that it took three days to immortalize President Reagan upon his passing into eternity as 108,000 people visited his presidential library in Simi Valley, California, to honor him by touching his casket. And we all know that Donald Trump likes big numbers.

THE INVISIBLE INDIVISIBLE

One has only to go to the Antifa website to discover that the group is the antithesis of traditional American values. Under the headline "Expropriation and the Cooperative Economy," its declared purpose is "to carve out an autonomous territory, or to begin the revolutionary process, goods, land, and tools must be expropriated, or taken away from those who withhold them. We are striving towards a situation where necessities cannot be taken away from those who need them, but instead are shared with those who lack them."

They hate capitalism. Private property is evil to them and should be taken from those who have it and given to whomever those in power decide need it. Intellectual property does not exist, and the artists who create music, the software and hardware developers who create the guts of the latest mobile phone, and the chemists and biologists who find cures and life-extending answers to disease have no claim on the products of their labors in Antifa's universe. The answer they give to about everything starts with the philosophy of Marxism and the belief that outcomes must be equalized.

America is built on a very capitalist idea, that each of us is "endowed by their Creator with certain unalienable rights... life, liberty, and the pursuit of happiness." The premise that people are entitled to pursue happiness is a guarantee of not happiness but rather the ability to reach for it, in whatever form that might take for each person. This means that in America, and in capitalism that grew from our foundation, each person should be allowed to pursue opportunity equally, but the outcomes for each individual are by design unequal based upon their ability, work, choices, and, to some measure, luck or providence.

Antifa's members reject America's founding principles including capitalism because of our nation's history of slavery, its disenfranchised women, and its treatment of the native indigenous populations that were driven from land by European invaders. In this rejection, they attempt to undermine the legitimacy of the entire American experiment. They believe that all the property and wealth accumulated over the past 500 years since Christopher Columbus first set foot in the Western Hemisphere is ill-gotten and should be given to all those who have been left behind.

Ideas of Marxism poured through taxpayer-funded public schools and universities have embedded in our youth to produce movements like Antifa. Protesters of the 1960s became the university professors of the eighties and trained the current crop of America haters. These ideas of the left rooted in Marxism are why they believe that capitalism must be destroyed. Those who have created immeasurable wealth not only for themselves but for the entire world are declared oppressors, and denying them the comforts associated with the fruits of their labor is not only justified but imperative.

But it is America that instituted a system of government that resulted in ever-increasing suffrage and wealth for those who were previously excluded. It is the virtues of capitalism that uniquely allow someone to rise from utter poverty to a station in the middle, upper middle, or even top of the economic heap based upon their own ability and initiative. Why? Because ultimately it is in the interests of the capitalist society to have the cream rise to the top regardless of gender or color while unfortunately it is in the interests of those who wish to control the means of production and to control the population with the honey of handouts to those who didn't earn them stolen from the wallets of those who did. This is yet another debate point that gave rise to the presidency of Donald Trump.

America has historically been the destination for people around the world who desired a better life for themselves not because of a desire to receive government-paid goodies but instead because of a desire to work for their own betterment with their own hands. They wanted the opportunity to till their own ground or start their own business or even work for someone else while giving their children the opportunity to advance their fortunes, ending generation after generation of poverty.

Rather than believing that America is a dream, the violent Antifa and Indivisible and their dangerous leaders like Bernie Sanders, Elizabeth Warren, and Kamala Harris believe that America is a nightmare that must be eradicated to be rebuilt into an idealistic Marxist utopia. After two generations of our youth being indoctrinated with Marx's philosophy, America now stands at a critical crossroads in clarifying the role of government with regard to capitalism and free markets.

We have reached a dangerous mass of dependency in our country of those who now have too much stake in big government, whether they are employed by it or collecting benefits from it or they are businesses getting favors from it, which is a fulfillment of Marx's dream without the gun.

The entire D.C. swamp is flooded with legislators, lobbyists, and lawyers to defend this status quo. Some call them the establishment. I call them the welfare state.

The political costs of communism's redistribution model in America now command a higher premium than freedom. The details of our $4 trillion federal budget are sickening. And hit hardest by the games inside the Beltway are entrepreneurs—the creators of tomorrow's ingenuity and jobs.

Through our tax system, politics in Washington has turned America into the land of the envious and the home of the victim. Washington, D.C., is producing millionaires while most small businesses are drowning in the red tape of excessive regulations and extreme taxation.

If Americans want prosperity, we need a grand reawakening to the fact that prosperity is fueled by entrepreneurs unfettered by meddling politicians. That communism is the enemy of freedom while capitalism is its energy.

We as a nation should engage again in the belief that capitalism should be embraced, not envied, because capitalism creates profits. And profit is good, moral, and necessary to help others as profit is the oil in the engine to create jobs.

#CAPPIEHAPPY

There are three big reasons why I believe capitalism should be embraced and not vilified.

1. Capitalism is good for entrepreneurs.

Apple Inc. is now the most valuable company in the world. I will talk about this in more detail later in the book, but here is one point about its founder's attitude.

Twenty years ago, in 1997, when Steve Jobs returned as CEO of Apple, the company was worth less than $3 billion, about half a percent of what it is worth today. Estimates then were that Apple was several months away from bankruptcy.[7]

John Lilly, a former Apple employee and now a Silicon Valley venture capitalist, blogged after Jobs's death about a talk that Jobs gave to employees shortly after his return. Apple was losing money, its stock was languishing, and there were rumors about the company being acquired, so Jobs was asked about a suggestion that the company just shut down. Jobs responded, "If you want to make Apple great again, let's get going. If not, get the hell out."

Capitalism is not about being on your own as we hear so often from LWLPs. Capitalism is about entrepreneurs being free to create prosperity by serving their fellow citizens with innovative ideas and products. And it's about government doing its proper job—protecting life and property—so this can happen.

According to the Kauffman Foundation, which specializes in studying entrepreneurship, almost all net new jobs created in our country come from firms less than five years old. Net new job growth in America comes from entrepreneurs—not from government bureaucrats and not even from corporate monoliths. And this entrepreneurial activity takes place at considerable risk.

According to one study from Case Western Reserve University, only 30 percent of new business start-ups are still operating after ten years. Entrepreneurs start and build their businesses with personal savings, credit cards, funds from family and friends, and loans and investments from banks and venture capitalists. Who would take these risks if success is punished rather than rewarded?

What entrepreneur will take these risks if power-seeking politicians get to decide that certain successful entrepreneurs have become too wealthy?

2. Capitalism is good for African American advancement.

According to a survey commissioned by Uber, 24 percent of its drivers are black. I use Uber all the time and meet these young black drivers, making extra money and building their entrepreneurial skills. Uber, the ride-hailing company founded in 2009, began operations in San Francisco in 2011 and now has a presence in more than 450 cities worldwide. From Uber's beginning with just a vision, the firm's market value now exceeds $60 billion, and in 2019 it introduced an initial public offering (IPO). Uber is just one of many emerging businesses that are the result of applying new technology to the routine affairs of living.

Using government to protect the status quo from competition is not in anyone's interest. Certainly not the interests of low-income Americans who want to get ahead. A 2015 report from the School of Business at the University of California, Riverside, notes that the number of black-owned businesses grew 40.3 percent from 2007 to 2012 compared with 3.4 percent of all businesses. The last thing these new black entrepreneurs need is to be regulated out of business. What we should have learned from both slavery and Jim Crow is that force is not an American value. Yes, it is true that when existing businesses find themselves threatened by innovation, they have only three choices: adapt and change, go out of business, or try to destroy the innovation that is challenging their existence.

I hang around a lot of lobbyists during my time in D.C., and most of them now dependent on government spend most of their professional time on the third option. America should be welcoming innovation, not sitting by complacent while a new generation of Marxist radicals try to crush it. A country obsessed with envy and redistribution laws has no future.

3. Capitalism is good for middle-class morale.

During days of welfare reform in the mid-nineties, one rally cry of then-Senator Phil Graham to help keep us focused on the goal was "I've never seen a man wash a rented car!" His point was that ownership builds morale and opportunity. And morale is good for middle- and low-income workers. Morale is why we need personal retirement accounts in Social Security reform. Morale is why we need work requirements and time limits in welfare reform. Morale is why we need educational and housing flexibility and mobility availed to our nation's poor. And, frankly, morale is one reason why we need to end legalized abortion, which I will also explain later. The truth is that a capitalist economy expands and contracts on cycles with the net result being an overall increase in wealth. And wealth is a good thing.

Since the dawn of the twentieth century alone, Americans went from an agrarian economy to an industrial economy to a services-based economy. In 1900, electricity was a new technology still being developed by Thomas Edison as a commercially viable product, and most Americans used outhouses. In spite of two World Wars, a Great Depression that lasted more than a decade, and the Great Recession in 2007 when the U.S. GDP grew even less than during the Depression, Americans not only have electricity, running water, and indoor toilets, but a 2017 Pew Research Center study reported that roughly three-quarters of Americans (77 percent) now own a smartphone.

The incredible increase in wealth that capitalism brings to the world is also seen worldwide, where both Statista and CBS report that the number of cell phones worldwide has hit 4.6 billion. The point that is missed by those who attack capitalism is that in the capitalist-dominated twentieth century, toilets and clean sanitation became commonplace all over the world with more than 60 percent of the world having access to them. The socialists and communists of the world had little to do with these amazing accomplishments.

The world is wealthier, and by and large even the poorest of the poor have been beneficiaries, not because of redistribution of wealth but because capitalism needs expanded markets for its goods and services, so increasing wealth all over the world is good business. Those who wish to redistribute wealth at the point of a gun have consistently succeeded only in enriching those who hold the gun while impoverishing their people, as we are witnessing in modern-day Venezuela, where pets have become food. Those who have embraced markets and free enterprise have prospered beyond imagination and in doing so have dragged the rest of the world with them. The ability to move massive numbers of poor people out of their poverty is why capitalism is the only moral economic system in the history of the world, and everywhere that has embraced even semblances of it has seen their overall economic fortunes increase.

While the temptation is to laugh at the ignorant college graduates who attack America as illegitimate and capitalism as evil as they drink a five-dollar cup of socially responsible coffee and use their mobile devices to communicate their revolution from the local Starbucks, it is important to remember that they are both deadly serious about transforming America and growing in numbers. The political class in Washington vested with the responsibility to protect capitalism had effectively ceded ground to them by agreeing with their redistribution agenda. Another reason the heartland elected businessman Donald Trump.

> The inherent vice of capitalism is the unequal sharing of blessings; the inherent virtue of socialism is the equal sharing of miseries.
>
> —WINSTON CHURCHILL

CHAPTER SIX

A Constitution on Life Support

T HE ELECTION of Donald Trump immediately led to a reaction from a wave of leftists determined to "resist" his presidency, attacking those who even considered that the forty-fifth president was legitimate.

Justifying their actions by their false belief that Trump was in some way so abhorrent to the American ideal that he could not be accepted under any circumstances, millennials and Obama supporters in the D.C. bureaucracy and academia were most attracted to #resist, with even Hillary Clinton joining the movement after previously conceding her defeat.

But millennials, traditional Democrats, and the LWLPs weren't the only ones in shock at Trump's election. Millions of Bible-believing, born-again Christians were also questioning the victory of a president with an extremely colorful past and personality of an enraged bully.

FOR MILLENNIALS, COULD QUESTIONING TRUMP'S PRESIDENCY BE ROOTED IN IGNORANCE?

More Americans are going to and graduating from college now than at any time in the history of the country, yet knowledge about basic U.S. history facts among college seniors is startlingly absent.

At least one could reasonably draw this conclusion after looking at the results of a 2015 survey of college graduates by the American Council of Trustees and Alumni, where 71.6 percent of recent college graduates could not identify James Madison as the father of the Constitution in a multiple-choice format.

In 2012, 83 percent of respondents failed to agree that Abraham Lincoln's Emancipation Proclamation stated that slaves were free in areas of the Confederate states not held by the Union, instead preferring the answer that slavery was abolished in the Union. In a 2016 report, 37 percent of those surveyed didn't know that presidential elections are held every four years.

A similar study conducted twelve years earlier by the same group focusing only on college seniors set to graduate from prestigious universities found similarly disturbing results, with 43 percent identifying Lincoln's Gettysburg Address phrase "government of the people, by the people, for the people" as coming from the Declaration of Independence. The same question asked in the 2012 survey showed the number who identified the phrase as being from the Declaration of Independence climbing to 54 percent. A 2016 report revealed that 9.6 percent of recent college graduates surveyed believed that television personality Judge Judy had been on the Supreme Court.

The sad truth is that college history majors may not even take an American history course during their matriculation. According to another report by the American Council of Trustees and Alumni (ACTA), 70 percent of the 76 colleges and universities ranked most highly by *U.S. News and World Report* do not require students seeking a history degree to take courses in American history. Further, a 2017 study found that only 17.6 percent of American universities require the completion of an American history or government course for graduation for their general student body.[8]

Is it any wonder that a 2017 poll of 1,000 Americans on patriotism in America by the American Culture and Faith Institute found that the younger the American, the less likely that the person holds what have been traditionally seen as patriotic values?

We've been told for two decades that the Constitution is breathing and able to be interpreted with the changing times. Well, it seems to be running out of breath.

Here are the age breakouts for the thousand respondents asked to self-identify whether the following statements are a "completely accurate" description of themselves. Having received news from self-selected news feeds and Comedy Central with very little actual knowledge about America's historic freedom quests, is it really a wonder that many millennials reject the very concept of American exceptionalism—not to mention any connection to the rule of law rooted in the Constitution?

Description of Yourself	18–29	30–49	50–64	65+
Tolerant of Different Social/ Political Views	36%	27%	19%	22%
Feel Proud to Be an American	34%	42%	52%	64%
Want Government to Stay Out of Your Life	33%	28%	26%	27%
Your Political Views Are Clear and Unchanging	28%	25%	24%	34%
A Culture Warrior	21%	13%	8%	7%
Would Prefer to Live in Another Country	21%	10%	7%	2%
Always Trust Government to Do the Right Thing	13%	8%	7%	2%

Not until you're in the demographic of people fifty years old and over do you find a majority who "feel proud to be an American," with only one in three people ages eighteen to twenty-nine proud. Not surprisingly, about one in five youths between the ages of eighteen to twenty-nine would prefer to live in another country.

But there are reasons why they hold these views. People are what they consume, and after being exposed to classrooms of derision directed at their nation with no countervailing facts being presented, they have learned to reject America and our Constitution. They have no idea of what it is or the brilliance of the document itself in terms of power sharing and protection of individual rights and the rights of those who hold minority opinions.

So, for the ignorant, it is no different resisting a Japanese whale hunt than the breathing Constitution, but it is not the earnest, young, misguided resisters who are the immediate primary threat to the nation.

It is the embedded government bureaucrats at places like the Justice Department who are not ignorant and know exactly what resisting the duly elected president of the United States means. Guilt lies at the feet of our elected Congress.

The #resist movement rose up to delegitimize an elected president using any means possible, including subversion from within the executive branch, which is what we witnessed in 2018 out of the Justice Department, exposing unprecedented corruption throughout the entire administrative state. Merely eleven days after President Trump took office, the *Washington Post* reported:

> Less than two weeks into Trump's administration, federal workers are in regular consultation with recently departed Obama-era political appointees about what they can do to push back against the new president's initiatives. Some federal employees have set up social media accounts to anonymously leak word of changes that Trump appointees are trying to make.

But revelations that many of the top career attorneys at the Justice Department and FBI actively engaged in espionage on behalf of the Clinton campaign and also ran an active campaign designed to drive President Trump from office signaled the real intent of the #resist movement: to end Constitutional governance and ensure that LWLPs maintain the power to transform America regardless of whom the people elect.

Maybe those #resist supporters who said when polled that they would prefer to live in another country should consider Venezuela, as its style of government might be a better philosophical fit. Or Egypt.

In case you have doubt that there is a concerted effort in our nation to overthrow our founding principles and doctrines at the highest levels of left-wing thought, consider this from Supreme Court Justice Ruth Bader Ginsburg, who told an Egyptian television audience that the U.S. Constitution should not be a model for Egypt's new government because it is "a rather old constitution."

Instead Ginsburg pointed to the more than 100-page constitution of South Africa based upon its newness. She totally ignored the uniqueness of the U.S. Constitution, which in its brevity and relative simplicity lays out the foundation for government and the freedoms of individuals from that government.

Ginsburg's choice is a proscriptive constitution that imbeds policy choices into the document rather than one that establishes individual freedom from federal government encroachment as the dominant and elegant value.

The Antifa movement supporters, along with the other #resisters, reject the validity of the Constitution and its framers, and as a result, the idea of having a proscriptive governing document that makes any election meaningless is far preferred.

For Ginsburg, for those of Antifa and Indivisible, and for many academics and government bureaucrats to engage in an attempted coup against our duly elected American president of the United States, there is no excuse.

While many of their millennial followers may be ignorant to what they are doing, the LWLPs are not. They know that they are sowing the seeds for the elimination of individual freedom, and it is they who must be #resisted.

FOR CHURCHGOERS, COULD QUESTIONING TRUMP'S PRESIDENCY BE ROOTED IN FEAR?

I understand the shock. President Trump's life choices, polemic personality, and temperamental Twitter habit defy the very pursuits of perfection Bible believers attempt to realize in their day-by-day decisions and dedication to follow Christ.

The Christian worldview is a desire to be holy as Christ is Holy (1 Peter 1:16). It is a lifetime of expressing love in our actions toward each other and our neighbors, friend or foe, because God first loved us (1 John 4:11). It is reaching to do the best we can do with our time, talents, and treasures for all the mercy given to us (Romans 12:1). It is at least trying to be an example of Christ in our private and professional lives so others will be attracted to Him (John 13:15).

Donald Trump's life choices reflected many of the choices Christians are to abhor. Christians are commanded to work out personal salvation with fear and trembling, and it doesn't make this hard task any easier when a wealthy secularist flaunts debauchery and celebrates lusts of the flesh in the public square. And for one of such flowery disposition to hold what some consider the most sacred seat of power in the world? I was as perplexed during the primaries as were many very credible Christian leaders whom I adore and as were many who sat in the Sunday-morning pew next to me. What was God doing? Didn't He see that American Christians were under tremendous attack from LWLPs and rapidly sliding into the type of persecution we try to rescue our fellow believers from in foreign lands? Was God not heeding our prayers for righteousness and justice and peace to flow through our land?

There were two scriptures that kept me, as a media pundit, silent after the Republican primaries and the GOP convention that declared Donald Trump its presidential candidate for 2016. The Democrats hadn't had their convention yet to choose Hillary Clinton over Bernie Sanders, but it was clear that would be the reality. Scriptures I

pondered included, first, Proverbs 25:2, the admonition of King Solomon that when God seems hidden, we are to reach deeper to find
Him. (The literal NKJV reads, "It is the glory of God to conceal a
matter, But the glory of kings is to search out a matter.) And, second,
I pondered Proverbs 21:1, also about King Solomon, which says in the
NKJV, "The king's heart is in the hand of the Lord, like the rivers of
water, he turns it wherever He wishes." Yes, I consult King Solomon
often, upon every personal crisis and professional dilemma, and actually I try to read one chapter of Proverbs every day to keep the devil
away. I think that was the intention of exactly 31 chapters, one for
each day of most months.

As I continued my work in D.C. and around the country on matters of culture, poverty, and building race relations, in addition to
contemplating these two proverbs right up until election night, there
were two other things that kept me motivated by the belief that God
was in control of the political moment of November 2016.

The first was my own personal testimony. From a youth who
engaged in criminal activity, drug activity, and sexual promiscuity
that led me in and out of abortion clinics to landing on welfare where
God found and rescued me, who was I to judge His intentions for
Donald Trump? I know firsthand not only that God can turn hearts
but also that one can look for Him and find Him even when He is
better at hide-and-seek than any kid who ever played the game. Sec-
ondly, I knew the story of Joseph.

I knew several very prominent leaders and personal friends who
believed that Trump was chosen and were adamant that he would
become resident, and I had heard about a book on King Cyrus called
God's Chaos Candidate, in which its author, Lance Wallnau, had made
a first-class case that Donald Trump was selected by God for this
American moment in history and would be president. But I work in
Swampland, so I heard these things from a distance and thus chose to
bury my head in my pillow on election night after a simple prayer that
joy would come in the morning. My hope that night that mercy would
be bestowed upon our country rested in the biblical story of Joseph.

Joseph, after being tapped by God for a very unique leadership role and purpose for his people, was sold into slavery at the hands of his brothers, was thrown in prison at the hand of his master for something he didn't do, was brought out of jail at a time of great turmoil for the pharaoh who needed him, and ended up as his right-hand man. For me, Joseph lived under circumstances very similar to America's current political reality, and in my estimation, the invisible hand in Joseph's story was embodied in Donald Trump's right-hand man, Mike Pence.

According to the biography of our amazing vice president on whitehouse.gov:

> Michael Richard Pence was born in Columbus, Indiana, on June 7, 1959, one of six children born to Edward and Nancy Pence. As a young boy he had a front row seat to the American Dream. After his grandfather immigrated to the United States when he was seventeen, his family settled in the Midwest... Sitting at the feet of his mother and his father, who started a successful convenience store business in their small Indiana town, he was raised to believe in the importance of hard work, faith, and family.
>
> Vice President Pence set off for Hanover College, earning his bachelor's degree in history in 1981. While there, he renewed his Christian faith which remains the driving force in his life.

I actually met Sarah B., a classmate at Hanover who told me many of the details surrounding Mike's recommitment story, when I recently stayed at her bed and breakfast in Kentucky.

> He later attended Indiana University School of Law and met the love of his life, Second Lady Karen Pence.
>
> After graduating, Vice President Pence practiced law, led the Indiana Policy Review Foundation, and began hosting *The Mike Pence Show*, a syndicated talk radio show and a weekly television public affairs program in Indiana. Along the way he became the proud father to three children, Michael, Charlotte, and Audrey.

In 2000, Mike launched a successful bid for his local congressional seat, entering the U.S. House of Representatives at the age of forty, which is when I first met him and when we became fast friends. I have adored and trusted him ever since. I, like many others close to him, knew that he, like Joseph, was tapped by God for a very special and unique leadership role and purpose for his people. In 2013, Mike Pence left our nation's capital when Hoosiers elected him the fiftieth governor of Indiana. In July 2016, GOP presidential front-runner Donald Trump selected Mike Pence as his running mate. I will let a few of his personal quotes explain why I'm so deeply dedicated to him as a modern-day Joseph and why I have assurance that we will be just fine as a country under the leadership of Donald Trump.

Words from Vice President Mike Pence on his White House Website:

"I believe in servant leadership, and the servant always asks, 'Where am I needed most?'"

"And my Christianity, first and foremost, governed the way that I tried to deal with people."

"Hoosiers don't believe in discrimination."

"The conservative movement today is like that tall ship with its proud captain: strong, accomplished but veering off course into the dangerous and uncharted waters of big government republicanism."

"In my home state of Indiana, we prove every day that you can build a growing economy on balanced budgets, low taxes, even while making record investments in education and roads and health care."

"I think it's time for the media and our leaders to get real and start telling the truth about the impact of adultery on our national life."

"I promise you that when the circumstances arise where I have a difference on policy or on presentation, I have—I

> can tell you in my heart, I know—I would have no
> hesitation, were I privileged to be vice president, to walk
> into the president's office, close the door, and share my
> heart."[9]

American Christians have always been at the forefront of resisting tyrannical government, not out of disdain for the Constitution and the rule of law but instead out of respect for and defense of it. The irony of the entire welfare state from the perspective of millennial activists of the left or churchgoers of the right is that statism ultimately preserves the power of the federal government, and in doing so, both special interest groups of LWLPs and the religious right are in league with the swamp creatures who are the primary beneficiaries of big government.

Thus, I could never be a never-Trumper, as the philosophy of big government stands against my worldview whether the case for it comes from the right or from the left. For me, the choice comes down to whom I will trust as final ruling authority: God or government. I agree with Dr. R. C. Sproul that these two cannot coexist as the ultimate agent of redemption. The two worldviews cannot be in control at the same time.

AMERICA DIVIDED AGAINST ITSELF, AGAIN

On May 22, 1856, Representative Preston Brooks entered the floor of the U.S. Senate, approached abolitionist Senator Charles Sumner, and beat the senator with a cane, almost taking his life.

Brooks was provoked by a passionate anti-slavery speech that Sumner had delivered in the Senate three days earlier, in which he assailed Senator Andrew Butler of South Carolina, a relative of Brooks, for his pro-slavery stance.

This sad and gruesome history is related on the website of the U.S. Senate, which concludes by saying, "The nation, suffering from the breakdown of reasoned discourse that this event symbolized, tumbled onward toward the catastrophe of the Civil War."

We ought to be concerned that again today the nation appears to be flirting with this uneasy territory where "reasoned discourse" is breaking down.

The president's then–press secretary, Sarah Sanders, was asked to leave a restaurant in Lexington, Virginia, where she was having dinner because, well, she works for Donald Trump.

Stephanie Wilkerson, owner of the Red Hen restaurant, said she asked Sanders to depart because "there are moments in time when people need to live their convictions. This appeared to be one."

But what exactly are the "convictions" that Ms. Wilkerson was living in this incident? That you refuse to talk, associate, or do business with anyone you disagree with? This is America?

A few days before, then–Homeland Secretary Kirstjen Nielsen had been harassed in a D.C. restaurant and then at her northern Virginia home. Longtime Congressional Black Caucus member Maxine Waters followed suit, calling for all-out warfare on the Trump administration.

"If you see anybody from that Cabinet in a restaurant, in a department store, at a gasoline station, you get out and you create a crowd and you push back on them, and you tell them they're not welcome anymore, anywhere," Waters told a crowd in Los Angeles.

According to the vision statement of Waters's Congressional Black Caucus Foundation, "We envision a world in which all communities have an equal voice in public policy through leadership cultivation, economic empowerment, and civic engagement."

Another dose of LWLP hypocrisy.

Reasoned discourse can take place only between parties who share basically the same values and a similar worldview.

This is what broke America down in the 1850s and brought the nation finally to a horrible civil war. Reasoned discourse is not possible between someone who thinks it is acceptable for one race to be enslaved to another and someone who finds this abhorrent.

Lincoln reached into the Gospel of Matthew and prophetically observed, "A house divided against itself cannot stand." The worldviews of liberals and conservatives, Democrats and Republicans, secular humanists and Christians, regarding what America is about, regarding what life is about, are so entirely different that all common ground seems lost and we appear to have arrived again at the "breakdown of reasoned discourse."

Half the country is on one page and half on another. America is again a house divided against itself.

I am certainly not predicting another civil war. But I am predicting that the kind of civil discourse that is essential for a country like ours to function as intended is becoming increasingly impossible and something will have to give.

Florida's Republican Attorney General Pam Biondi required a police escort to protect her from screaming thugs while exiting a movie theater in Tampa, Florida. White House advisor Stephen Miller was called a "fascist" while eating in a Mexican restaurant in Washington.

We may not be in a hot war. But we are certainly in a cold war.

The election of Donald Trump was about pushback. He himself is regularly criticized for lack of civility. But maybe this is partly why he won. He understands that today this is the game.

The Trump presidency opened the debate of whether those who believe in the cause of individual liberty, natural rights, and nature's God will allow themselves to remain in fear of the intellectual and physical thugs who permeated our government, commerce, media, academia, and the church with lies of a secular utopia of Marx philosophy, lies that our Constitution is racist and needs to be replaced by communism.

Will Christian freedom lovers rise with the Trump occasion to fight for individual liberty and protect our Constitution?

Members of the left have proven that they are deadly serious about dismantling our constitutional protections in order to completely transform America into a country without God and without capitalism. The tolerance movement in our society today warring against our culture, our capitalism, and our very Constitution is the grandchild of a diversity movement birthed by the feminist movement that piggybacked the civil rights movement. It is one part of a unified destructive movement driven by an embedded and emboldened totalitarian worldview.

But I must say here that this totalitarian diversity movement always demands tolerance and capitulation and is extremely and vilely intolerant toward anyone and everyone who does not conform to its LWLP worldview.

Could it be that the Trump phenomenon was birthed of providential mercy to awaken the fearful and the comfortable for one more chance for America not to simply fall by default?

The greatest threat to mankind and civilization is the spread of the totalitarian philosophy. Its best ally is not the devotion of its followers but the confusion of its enemies. To fight it, we must understand it.

—AYN RAND, *The Only Path to Tomorrow*, 1944

CHAPTER SEVEN

New Sexualized Culture Plays House

The survivors who are left from the captivity in the province
are there in great distress and reproach.

—Nehemiah 1:3 (NKJV)

T HE WALLS of America are broken down, and her gates are
burned with sexual fire.

Six adopted children dead. Driven over a cliff in California. Three
of the children were siblings who had been removed from their home
in Houston where they lived with their aunt. They had been temporarily placed with their aunt after their mom, who was struggling
with drug addiction, lost custody. Their auntie came to the rescue
them and began to raise them as her own.

The home was stable, their grades were going up in school, and
according to news interviews with their aunt, they were settled and
content. Some would think this was an incredible victory opposite
what had become an all-too-common outcome for the black children
disproportionately represented in our foster system: crime, drugs,
prostitution.

Their auntie, Priscilla Celestine, was jubilantly awaiting final
adoption approval when one day she had to work overtime and called

their mom to babysit. That's the day the social worker showed up. Court orders said that the mom was not to be near her children.

The three siblings, Devonte, Jeremiah, and Ciera, were immediately removed from their home in Houston, placed back into America's foster system, and then shipped to Minnesota to be adopted into a new family.

One problem: It wasn't a family at all. They were transported and adopted into a social experiment. Their new home was headed by two women, married according to America's new marriage definition declared by the U.S. Supreme Court in a 5–4 decision called *Obergefell v. Hodges.*

On June 26, 2015, the Supreme Court had ruled that the Fourteenth Amendment to the Constitution requires a state to license a marriage between two people of the same sex when their marriage was lawfully licensed and preformed out of state, legalizing same-sex marriage in the United States.

The six Hart children who died when their new family drove them off of a 100-foot cliff 180 miles north of San Francisco were severely malnourished, neglected, and abused, welfare records revealed.

Child protection officers began investigating Jennifer and Sarah Hart, both 38, as far back as 2013 when the six adopted children, biological siblings Jeremiah, Ciera, Devonte and biological siblings Hannah, Markis, and Abigail, were between eight and fifteen years old.

Five of the six children were so small in 2013 that their heights and weights were not listed on growth charts for children their age; in fact, some reports say they were half normal weight.

But every time a neighbor or a school official or the law tried to intervene, the lesbian women claimed that racism and homophobia were driving the accusations as they chose small, predominately white communities in which to set up shop in all three states where they took their adopted black kids to live: Minnesota, Washington, and eventually Oregon, where they resided when this horrible crime and tragedy occurred.

On March 2018, their nightmare ended in the Pacific Ocean, but the next day a nightmare began for Devonte, Jeremiah, and Ciera's Aunt Priscilla. She had become one of the latest countless victims of America's new social experiment of its new liberated and sexualized culture.[10]

OLD SCHOOL

There was a time when America seemed so innocent when talking, or, should I say, *whispering*, about sex. Blushing, we would explain sex to our children in metaphors like the birds and the bees. We dared not show Ricky and Lucy Ricardo in the same bed. Sex discussions with adults would result in shooing our children out of the room because they didn't need to hear "grown folks talk."

Public discussions of sex no longer have these kinds of moral parameters in America. Even so-called family television time must be closely monitored or there won't be enough time to rescue your children from a full rant of profanity or a semi-guarded sex act on your television screen.

Semi-guarded because only a strategically placed sheet shields the viewer from a tantalizing sexual encounter between a man and a woman. Sexual innuendo is interjected in the marketing of everything from candy to shampoo to cars.

Living in America's new sexualized culture, I have personally felt the need for a shower after many flights since the airlines have installed movies to view at every seat. Especially when I'm stuck in a middle seat. Once I sat between a white couple as the wife at the window seat watched a very sexually vivid chick flick while her husband sat on the aisle watching a sexually vivid black flick that not ten years ago would have been rated X.

Today, although making up only an estimated 3.8 percent of the American population, same-sex couples are showing up in everything from sitcoms to commercials to dramas to home shows to reality television shows and also in children's programming.

Just when you thought it was safe to sit your little one in front of the television set for innocent programming, Disney cartoon *Doc McStuffins*, a show marketed for preschool-age children, features lesbianism as normal family living.

Wow, we have come a long way, baby. And the noise surrounding this public sexual drama cannot be blamed on President Trump.

Prior to the sex research, sex studies, and introduction for a new social order of sexualized liberation, American sexual culture was based in personal restraint, self-discipline, and privacy.

Back in the day, children didn't know what their parents were doing after they fed them and put them to bed. All they knew was that every twelve months or so they were having a new brother or sister.

Dr. Judith Reisman points the finger at whom she describes as one mad scientist who unleashed this plague of public sexual discussion, corruption, and contagion on America in 1948, a man named Dr. Alfred Charles Kinsey.

NEW SCHOOL

Dr. Alfred Charles Kinsey was an American biologist, professor of entomology and zoology, and sexologist who in 1947 founded the Institute for Sex Research at Indiana University, previously known as the Kinsey Institute for Research in Sex, Gender, and Reproduction. He is best known for writing *Sexual Behavior in the Human Male* and *Sexual Behavior in the Human Female*, also known as the *Kinsey Reports*.

One of America's most controversial figures of the twentieth century, Alfred Charles Kinsey is credited through his studies of male and female sexual behavior with helping usher in the sexual revolution of the 1960s and 1970s. Kinsey's research on human sexuality opened national discussions in America's public square about the wide divide between sexual norms and narratives of the 1940s generation and his personal taste for sexual experimentations outside conjugal marriage.

Research done by Dr. Judith Reisman for one of several biographies on Kinsey revealed that "Kinsey had had affairs with men, encouraged open marriages among his staff, stimulated himself with urethral insertion and ropes, and filmed sex in his attic."[11] Today, much revelation of Kinsey's style of research regarding his staff would make even Harvey Weinstein blush with jealousy.

A self-proclaimed atheist and bisexual, Kinsey had a set of assumptions that human sexuality was subjective and should not be suppressed by restraints regarding age, gender, or species; thus, he spoke openly about prepubertal orgasms and bestiality. Questions still linger today as to whether Kinsey was a liberator or simply a well-learned, well-polished pervert.

In her 2010 book *Sexual Sabotage*, Dr. Reisman walks readers step-by-step through what she considers a fraud of the Greatest Generation that Dr. Kinsey would declare the men and women of that generation hypocrites of their sexual narrative.

Hypocrites to what? To the sexual narrative that the majority of men and women of the Greatest Generation held true to personal restraint, sexual discipline, and privacy? Then how does one explain the baby boom that followed the solders' return if they and their wives were sexually dipping elsewhere?

First, Kinsey reveals that according to his research, everyone was doing it, young and old, married and unmarried, and that most humans were suppressing urges that needed to be released, restraint stemming from a Victorian culture of sexual repression. So, which was it? Someone should have asked the sex expert why he asserted that members of the Greatest Generation were sexually trapped in Victorian chains yet that all were doing it.

Kinsey implicated all of the men and women of his generation as hypocrites because he suggested that they too had his impulsive inclinations:

> [I]t is probable that half or more of the boys in an uninhibited society could reach climax by the time they were three or four years of age, and that nearly all of them could experience such a climax three to five years before the onset of adolescence.
>
> —ALFRED KINSEY, Male volume, page 178

Kinsey claimed on one hand that both men and women were suppressing their sexual urges, but on the other hand he claimed that research revealed that, especially in the married generation of World War II, both the males and the females were violating fidelity. He purported that his studies showed that the married men and women of the Greatest Generation were actually sexually immoral, promiscuous, and deviant.

SUSPICIOUS MINDS

Fast-forward twenty years and Elvis Presley is recording what became a phenomenal hit called "Suspicious Minds." In the 1969 song, the lyrics lure the listener into the challenges of blind love amid the possibility of adultery. Caught in a trap between trust and truth. Yep, throw a little suspicion into the rush of marital emotion and sexual passion and a door for new social experimentation opens for a sexual revolution of pornography, promiscuity, abortion, divorce, baby births outside marriage, and sex trafficking.

While Kinsey forgot to mention that much of his study was on prisoners and declared homosexuals or bisexuals like himself, marital suspicions grew as major news outlets reported his research as profound and credible in cover stories of *Life* and *Time* magazines.

The next thing America knew was she was in a new era of radical feminist rage.

Nope. The drive-by media recklessness that Rush Limbaugh defined a decade ago or what Donald Trump coined as "fake news" upon his election didn't start after his inauguration. Nor did liberal bias on university campuses.

In fact, according to Reisman, "riding on the financial support and seemingly impeccable credentials of the Rockefeller Foundation, the National Research Council, and Indiana University, Kinsey published his distorted data in *Sexual Behavior in the Human Male* in 1948 and *Sexual Behavior in the Human Female* in 1953 and, as his fans say, the world was never the same."

You may ask why I trust Dr. Reisman. Because Dr. Reisman has been studying Alfred Kinsey for forty years and I have known her for twenty. She is an incredible researcher and scientific advisor and has consulted to four U.S. Department of Justice administrations, the U.S. Department of Education, and the U.S. Department of Health and Human Services. Her scholarly findings have had international legislative and scientific import in the United States, Israel, South Africa, Canada, and Australia.

Reisman wrote *Sexual Sabotage* simply to set the record straight about Kinsey and to expose how his infamous research caused much of the sex crimes against humanity we are dealing with today. She also just wanted to correct the sexual reputation of America's Greatest Generation.

According to Reisman, "While our fathers and grandfathers fought WWII, and while our mother and grandmothers both overseas and on the home-front bore the burdens of war, Alfred C. Kinsey did not. Instead, when America entered the war December 7, 1941, the forty-one-year-old zoologist was an Indiana University teacher 'researching' human sexuality.

"Wrapping himself in the mantle of 'science,' Kinsey, a secret sexual psychopath, would project his own sexual demons onto the men and women appreciably called the Greatest Generation, the Americans who saved the world from Hitler's national socialism."

THE ACLU'S ADOPTION PLAYGROUND

Jennifer and Sarah Hart, after what would be their final visit from Child Protective Services, America's agency for protecting the most vulnerable of our children from abuse and perversion, drove their adopted children, two sets of children of color, off that beautiful California cliff to their death.

After years of complaints from the three siblings adopted out of Houston, one social welfare worker determined that the women looked "normal."

Their auntie Priscilla had rescued them from a bumpy childhood and had begun to offer them a bit of stability and biological love. When the aunt took up the offer to work an extra shift, she violated the rules of the pending adoption, and the state removed the kids from her care. She fought to get them back, but she lost custody to the Harts.

The Harts had adopted them through one of the many new types of private adoption agencies growing around the country in response to same-sex marriage and adoption law changes. Old adoption laws were geared toward heterosexual married couples who were fully vetted by credible and long-time adoption service providers such as Catholic Charities.

You see, until same-sex marriage was legalized, our nation's adoption services for children deemed wards of the state were navigated mostly through public–private partnerships between Child Protective Services and religiously affiliated nonprofit organizations such as Catholic Charities.

But, post–new school sexual order, the ACLU took up the cause of trying to close Catholic Charities adoption services agencies because they adhere to Catholic doctrine, which teaches that marriage is the permanent, loving union of a man and woman open to raising children.

The ACLU sued St. Vincent Catholic Charities and Michigan state agencies in September 2017 because the Catholic agency would not place children for adoption with same-sex couples, only with a married husband and wife.

The ACLU challenged the state's practice of contracting with private, religious-based agencies to place children and a 2015 law that allows these agencies to act in accordance with their religious beliefs.

The ACLU contended that the law allows religious agencies, such as St. Vincent, to exclude same-sex couples from adopting, alleging that it "reduces placement options for the most vulnerable children."

ACLU lawsuits expanded nationwide, and thus Catholic Charities adoption services agencies, founded more than a century ago, began to be replaced in many states by small adoption agencies like the now-defunct Permanent Family Resource Center, founded in 2000.

The unreligiously affiliated one in Fergus Falls, Minnesota, in an unprecedented six months awarded adoption of Devonte, Jeremiah, and Ciera, and they joined three other vulnerable black children adopted by the Harts.

PRIVATE VERSUS STATE

The LWLPs must be related to Kinsey in that they love reversing roles. Everything is the opposite with them. They don't want traditional marriages, but they want children. As a result, big battles are ensuing in various states because state governments have been working with private religiously affiliated organizations such as Bethany Christian Services and Catholic Charities to help with foster and adoption services. For the past generation, these services have been contracted out by local governments to these adoption agencies with a general understanding that the best place for children is in a loving family with a married mom and dad. But since marriage laws changed to include same-sex couples, state family services laws are changing, which affects children in state custody. The push of the LGBTQ lobby has been to change state laws to accommodate homosexual adoption.

To counter this, religiously based groups have organized to protect the religiously affiliated groups from having to adopt children into homosexual households. Nine states have enacted measures that protect the rights of agencies to abide by their religious or moral convictions in adoption and foster care. They are Alabama, Kansas, Michigan, Mississippi, North Dakota, Oklahoma, South Dakota, Texas, and Virginia. But state legislation has not been enough to stop the LGBTQ lobby from demanding that all adoption agencies receiving state funding allow same-sex couples to adopt. Nine states have laws that require child welfare agencies to place children with same-sex couples in adoption, foster care, or both, according to Reuters

News Service. They are California, Maryland, Massachusetts, New Jersey, Nevada, New York, Oregon, Rhode Island, and Wisconsin. Catholic Social Services (CSS) brought suit after Philadelphia's Department of Human Services stopped cooperating with CSS and Bethany Christian Services because they refused to place children in same-sex homes. In another case, Catholic Charities of Fort Worth was sued for declining to place children with a same-sex couple.

So now religiously affiliated social services groups have organized to get the federal government to intervene. Legislation to prohibit government from discriminating against adoption and foster care agencies over their religious or moral convictions has taken an initial step toward potential passage in Congress. The proposal would bar the federal government—as well as any state or local government that receives federal funds—from discriminating against or taking action against a child welfare agency that refuses to provide services in a way that conflicts with its religious beliefs or moral convictions, such as placing children with same-sex couples. If enacted, the legislation would require HHS to withhold 15 percent of federal funds from a state or local government that violates its ban. The Southern Baptist Ethics & Religious Liberty Commission (ERLC) and other advocates for the bill have called for this federal solution to the growing pattern of state and local governments requiring adoption and foster care agencies to place children with gay couples or shut down such services.

Talk about expanded government! I spoke recently at a university where during the Q&A a young man confronted me about the inconsistency that I argue for smaller government and against public displays of homosexuality at the same time. He felt government should stay out of these questions of personal sexual morality. I had to remind him that it was the LGBTQ lobby that took its grievance to the government and expanded its role in these sexual matters. That most times these matters were put before the public to vote, the public voted on the side of privacy. A great irony of taking questions from college students is that on one hand their sign says "stay out of my bedroom" but while carrying the sign they used the other hand to invite the public into their bedroom when they changed state laws on marriage and family by appealing to the courts.

The religious communities are the one on the defense. It was the homosexual lobby that forced its agenda up through the courts. As one of my clergy friends said regarding this phase of the culture war, the difference between this sin and many other sins is that this sin hired a lobbyist!

I think the biggest problem for proponents of our new sexualized culture is that most Americans, particularly American parents of young children, believe that sexual behavior is adult behavior so it should be kept private. The ACLU and its LWLP cousins believe that all sexual behavior should be discussed in our schools with children as young as five. And this movement didn't start yesterday, as one of the first children's books with lesbian characters, called *Heather Has Two Mommies*, was published in 1989.

I hope you get the intensity of this conflict between the right and the left on matters of public morality and private behaviors. This part of the culture war gets really heated because for those that want to live devoutly and by the orthodoxy of the scriptures, the homosexual lobby is a real threat. If LGBTQ nondiscrimination laws keep encircling them in the public square, it's legitimate for them to ask society whether they can bring their beliefs outside. On the other side, for those who want to live outside biblical orthodoxy regarding sexual matters yet want acknowledgment in work, play, and family life, the question becomes whether both of these lifestyles can coexist without displacing the others' private choices. Donald Trump brought the opportunity for sex privacy advocates to get a boost toward pre-Kinsey American values regarding sexual discussions when he appointed several leaders to head major departments in his cabinet who understand the dilemma between the two sides yet align with the philosophy of limited and smaller government.

The reason I bring this up as an important component of this debate is because the smaller the government, the fewer opportunities for these two different bodies of Americans to be forced to share personal space. The public square is where our lives touch, and the challenge with big government is our lives are forced to touch in unnecessary spaces and places today. According to the Constitution, we each have a right of association. If we learn nothing else from our eras of slavery and Jim Crow, let us learn that force is not an American ideal.

I think far too many on the left don't know that America is a republic so the people get to decide on the values in the public square. And the country is designed so we battle our values in the voting booth. The left has gone to the courts to force its values for decades, and the heartland of America has had enough.

The election of President Trump was proof that many voters think that it is not up to the state to come into their homes through the public school system and demand that their children hear of sexual matters. The state can only come into one's home when a crime has been committed or is suspected, and even then, the state needs a warrant according to the Fourth Amendment to the U.S. Constitution. What the LWLPs did regarding public sexual discussions is go to the courts and pass laws that force the state into private homes and private businesses to demand that every American citizen discuss and embrace their sexual philosophies and proclivities. The fact that candidate Donald Trump provided a list of judges who he would consider for the Supreme Court if elected president assured more than a couple of voters that under the leadership of Donald Trump instead of Hillary Clinton, the left would not be playing house in their homes much longer.

CHAPTER EIGHT

Where Shall the Feminist Go Now?

And when you're a star, they let you do it. You can do anything.

—DONALD TRUMP, 2005

I did not have sexual relations with that woman, Ms. Lewinsky.

—BILL CLINTON, 1997

A FAMOUS FEMINIST slogan of 1975 had two versions: "A woman without a man is like a fish without a bicycle" or "A woman needs a man like a fish needs a bicycle." The point of the slogan attributed by Gloria Steinem to an Australian social activist was that woman is capable of living a complete and independent life without man. Look, I'm not going to pretend that I cannot relate to what life must have been like for women unable to vote or work her way to the top of a corporate ladder or women assumed to be the weaker sex who were good only for cooking, cleaning, and bedroom cruising. But come on, ladies: How far do we let the feminist movement take this thing? Fish might not need bicycles, but a man-less world would be quite boring.

For better and in some cases for worse, the feminist sexual revolution of the sixties and seventies has largely accomplished its stated
goal of leveling the playing field between the sexes, particularly in the
law and in the workplace. One measure is that the unemployment
rate for men and women remains virtually identical. Or worse might
be that men are now attending yoga classes and shaving their chests!

Male dominance in employment and business has so changed
since the sixties and seventies in that women make up 47 percent,
almost half, of the U.S. labor force today. In 2013, four in ten American households with children under age eighteen included a mother
as either sole or primary income earner for her family. According to
Pew research, of these breadwinning moms, 37 percent are married
moms who have higher incomes than their husbands. Truth that
seems to have escaped the feminist crowd is the Great Recession disproportionately impacted men, who bore the brunt of the economic
calamity dramatically due to their domination of fields like mining,
logging, construction, and manufacturing, while women working in
heavily female-dominated professions like nursing were significantly
less impacted as health care jobs continued to grow. The question of
whether a wage gap still exists in the workplace is subject to debate;
however, what is undeniable is that women have more career opportunities in the U.S. system of capitalism than anywhere else in the
world. Undeniably, an employer who discriminates against a highly
productive woman is much more likely to lose her as she finds work
in a place that will better appreciate her contributions of intellect
and hard work. The acceptance of women in leadership positions in
the workplace has become so pervasive that Americans felt comfortable rejecting the sexist argument that it was a woman's time to be
president.

Left-wing feminist leaders were shocked on the day after the
election that exit polls showed how white women had voted. They
were incredulous and angry that 53 percent of white women voters
had voted for President Trump, rejecting their insistence of a female
president simply because she was female. Astonishing to the radical

females who could only see gender, Hillary Clinton dramatically underperformed with her anticipated base, white women with college degrees, only winning 51 percent of their votes while she was overwhelmingly rejected by women without college degrees as Trump earned 62 percent of those votes. The rage on the left was palpable as feminist Sarah Ruiz-Grossman wrote in a *Huffington Post* article titled "Dear Fellow White Women: We F**ked This Up": "Fellow white women, I'm done with you."

A VAST RIGHT-WING CONSPIRACY

The lines could not have been clearer. Hillary Clinton was the ultimate expression of a hyphenated candidate, who explicitly ran as a woman—*I'm with her*—hoping to mobilize her gender in the way that President Obama mobilized African Americans in the previous two elections. And she failed spectacularly. It turns out that white women, particularly those not subjected to the four-year Ivy League indoctrination mills, did not buy into the disenfranchised, gender warrior stereotype their self-presumed leaders believed in so completely.

Rather than recognizing the failure to convince women to vote for Hillary and against Trump, the modern feminist movement had decided long ago that if it just engaged in a long, increasingly shrill scream of victimology, the public would give it anything it wanted just to shut it up.

Unmistakable are the visible hatred and vitriol levied against President Trump upon his presidential election victory. He promised some things in his campaign that if realized would leave feminists in quagmire. Radical feminists have invested their lives in a sexual revolution, to purge men from being male by purging women from being female. Now, in one election their dreams became a nightmare as, more often than not single and barren, they watch their sexual revolution backfire.

Radical feminism is based in and driven by a philosophy of

victimhood that believes men are the reason women are not equal to
them. Its followers believe that it is male supremacy that stands in the
way of their academic, social, and economic aspirations or capacities.
These women view American society as fundamentally patriarchal;
thus, they consider male dominance in all forms, whether personal
or professional, to be always oppressive to women. Deeply rooted
in this opinion, they invested all of their political chips to rail for
abortion and reproductive rights, assuming doing so would level the
playing field between genital differences. If all aspects of radical feminism were explored, the end results of the feminists' sexual revolution
and the role it played in current politics deserve some sympathy. The
courts meant everything to them, and because Hillary lost the presidential election, radical feminism lost the courts. Sixty-eight million
abortions since *Roe v. Wade* is a lot of personal investment and sac-
rifice for equality.[12] Donald Trump beat Hillary Clinton and could
have up to three appointments to the U.S. Supreme Court. Ouch.

Radical feminists have used the courts for four decades to secular-
ize America, and the 2016 presidential election declawed fifty years of
work. The genital differences they tried so hard to eliminate were up
front and embarrassingly amplified in the alpha male elected to the
presidency. Everybody knew that he was a man's man not just in his
posture but in his language. Trump's presidency was not just a repudiation for white males as the news media will have you believe as
they point to the voter demographics showing his big numbers among
white men. Trump reduced the feminist left to a pathetic national
temper tantrum largely because its positions were also rejected by a
wide margin of American white women. There are millions of American women who don't ascribe to the positions of the left, including
abortion. There are millions of married women and moms who think
about a lot more than so-called women's issues and whether it's a
woman's turn when they go into the election booth.

President Trump's election reduced the entire feminist movement
to clanking rage and bitter scorn. And his administration is working
tirelessly to reverse the scourge of abortion on our society and culture.

He has done much to support the unborn from encouraging the pro-life community by addressing its annual D.C. March for Life to appointing conservative judges to the courts. In addition, he has permitted states to defund Planned Parenthood of Title X funding; he has stopped tax dollars funding abortion overseas; he has defunded the pro-abortion UNFPA; he has required health insurance companies to disclose whether plans cover abortion; he has allowed states to defund Planned Parenthood of Medicaid funds; and he has cut Planned Parenthood federal tax funding by up to $60 million. The presidency of Donald Trump is exposing the utter disdain for traditional family life of radical feminists, and I believe his efforts will be rewarded in 2020 so he can continue to reverse their hostile takeover of our culture.

IT'S THE ECONOMY, LADIES

The idea that women are a voting bloc is repugnant to a vast swath of women who view life through differing experiences and lenses. This fact is seen as a betrayal by the highly educated elite feminists.

But the truth is that women without college degrees were left behind by the Bush–Obama new normal economy. Their families were disproportionately harmed by the hollowing out of rural America due to a combination of exported manufacturing jobs, the federal government's war on natural resource extraction and usage jobs, and a Hollywood culture that mocked them.

Rather than being solely driven by their genetic code as the leftist, gender identity crowd demands, women have demonstrated the capacity to make choices based upon their philosophies, economic and personal circumstances, and morals, just like any X-chromosome-bearing humans do.

Working women are the beneficiaries of lower unemployment rates, just as working men are. Black working women's unemployment rates have significantly declined, just as black men's unemployment rates have, impacting attitudes toward President Trump.

The far-left feminist challenge is that they have become effectively single-issue advocates due to their own victories on women in the workplace, and while polls show that a majority of women support abortion in some instances, they do not support abortion regardless of circumstance.

Much to the chagrin of LWLP feminists, women are more religious than men, and those women who regularly attend church are less likely to support abortion on demand.

The failure of Democrats and their feminist surrogates to hold President Bill Clinton accountable for his abominable Oval Office actions changed the attitude of what was once general American thought about acceptable behavior for those in public life, and President Trump was/is the beneficiary. If Monica was Bill and Hillary's business, then certainly some porn star who allegedly played sex games with the president ten years before he ran for president could only be considered Donald and Melania's business. For Hillary her husband's adultery was summarized as a vast right-wing conspiracy. So, for all we know the slogan "I really don't care. Do you?" on the green jacket Melania wore to visit immigrant children in Texas that received swarms of headlines may have been her modern-day, liberated woman's response to Stormy Daniels.

By the way, after two weeks of relentless media pundit pondering of what internal sentiment she might have been expressing, that jacket flew off the shelves of Zara, and knockoffs at other stores completely sold out. I know because I went to buy one and couldn't find one anywhere, not even online. As for Hillary and Bill, the vast right-wing is not a conspiracy at all but free individuals, both men and women, who know in their guts what they believe and want and don't need a bunch of angry outraged progressives telling them otherwise.

FISH WITHOUT A BIKE

The sophisticated college-educated females of the 1950s were trained to trust the sexual research of Alfred Kinsey. And they did.

Dr. Kinsey convinced massive numbers of young adults to be suspicious of each other sexually because, according to him, no human can totally escape sexual lusts and desire for exploration.

Fearfully in avoidance of pain that could result from adultery, the female children of the Greatest Generation—baby boomers—created a door to sexual freedom, normalizing open marriages, promiscuity, and no-fault divorce. The reason I implicate the women is that I believe in the saying "men will be men," and sexually, men will do almost anything for sexual gratification: marry and maintain fidelity or not marry and roam. I believe they'll do whatever the female wants because most men simply just want to please a woman. The suspicion of feminists that all men are dogs and none will be faithful only to leave women heartbroken fueled the feminist movement of the sixties. Instead of barefoot and pregnant, a liberated woman would be braless and barren. Instead of in the kitchen with apron and kids, into the boardroom she'd go in a pantsuit and with a briefcase.

But the reality ignored that has now boxed all women into trying to discover where we shall go post-feminist movement is that the female cycle related to gender differences that most feminists hate reminds women of childbearing age monthly that they are indeed women. A woman is not a man whether she has or doesn't have a corporate title or seat at the boardroom table. The great beauty of the female cycle is that woman is the one who holds the biological clock for mankind's future.

The irony is that radical feminism has let men off the marriage hook: as it became more and more culturally acceptable and pervasive that women were willing to abort their pregnancies and/or bear children outside marriage, advanced, advantaged, and powerful men were unleashed and empowered as *savage males*.

Men's participation in this sexual compromise, rejecting the requirement of marriage before any bedsheet motions, left millennials and Generation X exposed to the heartbreaking headlines of testosterone roller coasters Weinstein, Weiner, and Trump. What Billy Bush caught on tape was only a small glimpse into the world of a fish without a bicycle.

MATERIALISM TAKEOVER

It's hard to compare research on marriage and family life in the sixties with research on marriage and family life today and not see that as traditional family life declined our social problems and programs have expanded. Mountains of data shows that the sexual revolution has backfired. One glance through data at both Pew and Gallup will show you chart after chart to prove this point. In a sentence, the sexual revolution can be summed up as such: marriage is expendable, promiscuity expectable, abortion unhindered, births outside marriage acceptable, pornography mainstreamed, and the sex trafficking of children common worldwide. Our great challenge to course-correct these things is that we must first recognize the source of the conflict. The anti-marriage and family movement of the sexual revolution is a movement of materialism. Life is only and exclusively about me.

Abortion is a very messy and noisy battle in America's culture war and will remain such as long as it is legal and as long as Planned Parenthood insist on laws that grandparents have no voice in the matter nor do the dads of unborn children at death's door. Not only does abortion feed a narrative that women are victims of sexual impulses, but likewise it feeds the narrative of materialism. That life is about things I want and can get. It's why groups like National Right to Life and Susan B. Anthony are elated that both state and national abortion laws are changing because of President Trump's initiatives and tweets on the subject. Since his election, those in the abortion lobby have totally exposed themselves as supporters of late-term abortion and even infanticide. The more the debates over abortion are stirring in legislative sessions across the country, the more the nation gets to discover just how brutal abortion is. When New York celebrated signing infanticide into law, it brought the discussion into the headlines as a 2020 election issue.

The point is that what we lose in materialism is the wisdom of the ages, the wisdom that secures us in our present and our future. Wisdom is the truth conveyed from one generation to the next. It's the truth we don't discover in a laboratory. It's the truth and wisdom passed through families birthed in conjugal marriage. The arrogance of materialism is to say I am the center of the world and the point of my life is me. The supposed discovery of feminism turns out to be no discovery at all. What postures as new is really very, very old. What postures as the solution is really the problem.

It turns out that conjugal marriage and traditional family are not a natural state of affairs. That without the truth and wisdom of the ages, which teach us that every individual is a critical and vital part of the world but not the center of the world, conjugal marriage and traditional family disappear. The wisdom of Proverbs tells us that children are our future. Several years ago, Lord Jonathan Sacks, former chief rabbi of the United Kingdom, spoke at the Humanum colloquium on complementarity at the Vatican. He began his remarks, which received a standing ovation, by saying he would speak about "the most beautiful idea in the history of civilization: the idea of the love that brings new life into the world...Life begins when male and female meet and embrace"

But in the pride and arrogance of feminist materialism, which deny there are truth and wisdom that provide the tools to transcend the passion of the moment, marriage indeed becomes a political whim, children wallow, uncertainty expands, and our future disappears.

It's clear that this is what has happened in American culture as materialism has gradually but decisively taken over. In 1960, 72 percent of American adults over the age of eighteen were married. By 2016, this was down to 50 percent. In 2012, 20 percent of American adults over twenty-five, about 42 million Americans, had never been married. In 1960, it was 10 percent.

The National Center for Health Statistics reports that in 2016 American fertility reached a historic low—only sixty-two births per 1,000 women ages fifteen to forty-four. In 1960, our fertility rate was more than 120 births per 1,000 women. By the mid-seventies, it dropped precipitously to under seventy. Now, at sixty-two, we're at an all-time low.

Gallup has been surveying American opinion about ideal family size since the 1930s. From the early 1940s until the late 1960s, about 70 percent of Americans said that three or more children is ideal. By the late 1970s, it was down to 32 percent. Although in recent years its creeping back up—in 2018, 41 percent said the ideal family size is three or more children—it's still a little more than half of what it once was. Interestingly, the tendency of American women to not bring children into this world is skewed by race, which is now incredibly politicized due to different racial groups' perceptions on the role of government. According to Pew, 17 percent of white women between the ages of forty to forty-four are childless compared to 15 percent of black women and 10 percent of Hispanic women. Twenty percent of Hispanic moms have four or more children, 18 percent of black moms have four or more children, but just 11 percent of white moms do. Meanwhile, as the number of children Americans are bringing into the world is dropping, the percentage of children Americans are bringing into the world is increasingly outside the framework of marriage.

In 1960, 5 percent of births in America were to unwed mothers. Today, the rate is 41 percent. Much of the pushback from the Trump generation and why they supported him is rooted in a sense that something has been very wrong. That the takeover of materialism, that the takeover of feminism, that the trashing and marginalization of the values of our grandparents, that values on which America was built are bringing down our nation and our future. The collapse of family and the declining priority to bring children into the world mean a nation with an increasing percentage of elderly, which then creates new crises.

Take the crisis of our Social Security system, for instance. The checks that retirees get come from the payroll taxes that current workers pay. When FDR signed Social Security into law in 1936, there were around forty-five Americans working for every one retiree. Today this is down to three to one. In another twenty years, it will be two to one.

Health care costs for all of us go up as our population ages. Most health care expenditures are among the elderly. As the percentage of elderly increases, which is the result of not having children, the health care burden on the entire population increases.

And to top off the dilemma, lots of current data also show that poverty is disproportionately centered in single-parent households: the only female population group who didn't read the LWLP memo that *children are environmental hazards, so don't produce too many—if any.*

The administration of Donald Trump has thankfully begun the process of resetting the clock to stimulate not only our financial economy but also our cultural economy. Folks on the right still struggling with the reality of his presidency can rest assured on this extremely important point.

Many of the folks he has put in leadership in departments that influence our culture, like Health and Human Services, Labor, Housing, and Education, are quality conservatives who understand the urgency of reversing the damage feminism has done in our public square.

And the left knows this, which explains some of its screeching noise.

Sorry, feminists. You didn't discover anything new. You've been selling the country lies against the truth and wisdom that the ages have known for thousands of years.

Conjugal marriage not important? Traditional family not important? Men and women not different? It's just not true.

CHAPTER NINE

Gender-Neutral Identity Crises

S HE WAS transitioning to *he* while her partner, a man, was transitioning to become a *she*. Her name is Laura, and she lives in Oklahoma. Yep, it's okay that I call her *she* because Laura stopped taking meds to become a *he*. Only she had already gone so far into transitioning that although her feminine beauty was returning, her breasts never would.

And the left wonders why so many evangelical Christians overwhelmingly support Trump?

How are the caretakers of our moral code of ethics supposed to protect and secure the eternal, foundational truths of our society amid this type of cultural breakdown?

And CNN isn't helping. It is as if they are cultural warriors instead of objective journalists when they promote stories that have such wide implications on our society and culture.

A June 2018 CNN headline: "He gave birth. He breastfed. Now, he wants his son to see him as a man."[13]

Oh, the photo that accompanied the headline? It was of a baby boy in a diaper being held by the transitioned woman, who was wearing only pants so we could see that she had had her breasts removed in the process of becoming a man.

Upon viewing the photo, my heart sunk as I couldn't help thinking about the excruciating agony many women who I know have gone through when told their breast cancer recovery is dependent on a mastectomy. But now breast removal is a transitioning trend?

The CNN story:

Like many new dads, Sabastion Sparks knew parenting would come with serious challenges. But most new dads didn't give birth to their child. They didn't breastfeed them. And they don't endure glares from strangers when they go shopping with their wife and their toddler son.

Sabastion, 24, is a transgender man who lives with his wife Angel in suburban Atlanta. Assigned the female gender at birth, he began transitioning five years ago. It's a process that felt more complete last month when he had surgery to remove his breasts.

Sabastion Sparks gave birth to son Jaxen in October 2016.

With Father's Day approaching, Sabastion finds himself thinking about gender roles and what it means to be a dad. He wants Jaxen, their 20-month-old son, to have as normal a childhood as possible.

And for the first time, he now feels at ease inside his own body. He hopes Jaxen will see that difference.

Stories like these are why people like me applaud when President Trump tweets out about fake news because it seems CNN is celebrating as if there are not serious consequences and questions behind these cultural shifts.

Laura from Oklahoma had started thinking about her transitioning actions after listening to Dr. Everest Piper on the radio week after week on her drive to work. One day, she decided to go home, apologize to her mom and dad, and return to their church. Her former church embraced her, loved on her, and wept with her, and her pastor is helping her cope daily with what happened. When I first met Laura, she kept looking down as she talked and she kept joking about relearning to wear high-heeled shoes. She is a beautiful young woman, a little tomboyish, but it was evident by the shyness she exhibited that she was a vulnerable soul. She told me all about her childhood and when, why, and how she entered the world of gender confusion. She started crying when she spoke of her inability to ever be able to get her breasts back now that she is no longer a boy but back to being a girl. All I could do was hug her and cry with her.

GENDER REVOLUTION OR TRUTH REVOLT

A law firm in Alaska is now defending itself for taking on a case to protect a women's homeless shelter that did not want to take in a transgender man, the headline read. No sooner than the ink was dry on the Supreme Court determination of whether a baker could be forced to make a certain type of cake, our courts are getting busier by the day on these culture war questions. The Anchorage Equal Rights Commission (AERC) previously sued the Downtown Hope Center, a women-only homeless shelter, for not admitting a man who identified as transgender. *World Magazine* reported that on January 26, 2018, the local Anchorage police dropped off Timothy Coyle—who goes by Samantha Coyle—at the Hope Center, and it refused him not only because it is a women's homeless shelter and he is a man but also because Mr. Coyle was clearly under the influence of drugs or alcohol, which is against the Hope Center's rules. By February 1, Coyle filed a discrimination complaint with the AERC against the homeless shelter. Coyle defined himself in the complaint as female, transgender, and thus belonging to a protected class. The Hope Center then hired attorney Kevin G. Clarkson. Clarkson said in a letter he submitted to the commission that "[the Hope Center] does not shelter homeless men in its overnight shelter because this would traumatize and present unreasonable safety risks for the abused and battered women who are admitted for overnight shelter." On May 15, the AERC filed a complaint against Clarkson's law firm claiming that his comments violated the city's nondiscrimination law.

Unfortunately, this is a dilemma for many Christians serving the homeless in their local communities. This cultural conflict and the aggressiveness from the left against religiously affiliated Christian service providers cannot be denied. And it's important for me to single out the Christian service providers because the progressive purge movement is never directed toward Muslim or other religious minority service providers in America.

The dangers of recruiting children into discussions of sexual matters, especially in public schools, have been of great concern within America's Christian community for decades, yet they have been shouted down and mocked and Christians have been marginalized for even daring to raise any questions of long-term impact on individuals, much less our society.

Donald Trump's presidency has given these private service providers for the nation's most vulnerable a voice for their concerns and the societal costs associated with them by hiring people of the various civil rights agencies in each department to handle these various cases springing up all around the country. I have met some of the folks at the Offices of Civil Rights at HHS and Education and can assure you that they are well prepared for the task of protecting the interests of our nation's private service providers.

Our nation's orthodox communities understand deeply through the Bible that once barriers around human sexuality have been removed, our society will cease to be civil, so their role in our society must be protected. Moving beyond the Bible, even secular research not tainted by any hidden agenda of the researcher, as in the case of Kinsey, says mankind without a definitive framework for sexual behavior puts societies most tender, young, and innocent at risk to be lured into behaviors with significant risks to their health and well-being.

TRANSGENDER SUICIDAL CONCERN

An October 2017 issue of *Psychology Today* asks, "Why Are Suicide Rates Higher among LGBTQ Youth?" According to the Centers for Disease Control and Prevention, suicide is the second-leading cause of death among LGBTQ youth ages fifteen to twenty-four and the third-leading cause of death among LGBTQ youth ages ten to twenty-four.[14]

In a survey conducted by the National Center for Transgender Equality with the National Gay and Lesbian Task Force, 41 percent of respondents answered "yes" to the question "Have you ever attempted suicide?" Those who have medically transitioned (45 percent) and surgically transitioned (43 percent) have higher rates of attempted suicide than those who have not (34 percent and 39 percent, respectively). Cross-dressers assigned male gender at birth (biological males) had the lowest reported prevalence of suicide attempts among gender identity groups.[15]

General risk factors for suicide among the sexually confused have been speculated as a family history of suicide, childhood maltreatment, and having mental illness such as—in particular—borderline personality disorder, schizophrenia and psychotic disorders, antisocial personality disorder, conduct disorder, and depression, along with other factors. The fact that our society has recently so heavily encouraged homosexuality as an acceptable life choice offers little room for those challenged by their internal inclinations and struggles. It is one thing to personally struggle through each of our pulls toward questionable behaviors but quite another when a society ignores definitions of sin and endorses the behaviors.

ANTI-ORTHODOXY UNACCEPTABLE

The left's continuing efforts to try to mentally enslave blacks within liberal orthodoxy through gang tackling or outright destroy individuals who dared to think for themselves on matters of homosexuality were one major reason many black evangelicals joined white evangelicals in support of Trump's presidency.

The story of Kelvin Cochran clarified for them the reality of what was at stake.

Kelvin Cochran is a black, Christian male who rose from poverty to become the fire chief for the city of Atlanta. He was so widely respected across all political lines that after a year as that city's fire chief, he was asked to join the nascent Obama administration in 2009, was awarded National Fireman of the Year, and then went back to his old job in Atlanta with a unanimous confirmation a year later so his children could complete their schooling there.

Kelvin Cochran is a national jewel, known well as an impressive man of impeccable integrity, with an incredible personal story of escaping harsh racism and poverty growing up in the Jim Crow South. He is adored by his family and friends and admired by his peers, and the politicians of Atlanta knew it.

In late 2014, homosexual advocates found that Cochran had self-published a book called *Who Told You That You Were Naked?* for a men's Bible study class that he taught at his church. The book contained two mentions of homosexuality based upon his biblical truths about sexuality. For contextual purposes, here is the entirety of one "offending" page of reference terms and definitions:

Adultery—unlawful sexual relations between men and women, single or married, when one is married.

Fornication—same as adultery above besides all manner of other sexual relations.

Uncleanness—whatever is opposite of purity; including sodomy, homosexuality, lesbianism, pederasty, bestiality, and all other forms of sexual perversion.

Lasciviousness—licentiousness, lustfulness, unchastity (sexually suggestive), and lewdness (inciting to lust), wantonness (sexual lawlessness), and filthy; anything tending to foster sexual sin and lust.

The other reference to homosexuality that turned Chief Cochran's life upside down reads as follows:

Sexual acts pursued for purposes other than procreation and marital pleasure inside of Holy Matrimony is the sex life of a naked man.[16]

He argued that "when men are unrestrained in their quest for sex outside of God's purpose, they will never be fulfilled. Naked men refuse to give in, so they pursue sexual fulfillment through multiple partners, with the opposite sex, same sex, sex outside of marriage, and many other vile, vulgar, and inappropriate ways which defile their body-temple and dishonor God. This is the kind of sex that leaves a man continually empty—the sex life of a naked man. Who told you that you were naked?"

For those two mentions of God's truth about sexual sin and its corrosive nature on man, Atlanta Fire Chief Kelvin Cochran was fired.

Note that he did not single out homosexuality in particular, merely including it with adultery and other sexual behaviors, demonstrating the notion that sin is sin. Cochran was fired because he did not accept the position that homosexuality is acceptable in the eyes of God, and that made him an apostate for those who worship at the secular left's shrine.

In four short years, he went from the unanimous selection of the Atlanta city council to head its fire department to dismissal—a very public media event firing at that. All because he came out of the closet about his faith and called sexual sin, well, a sin.

His termination was because he declared that sexual activity and pleasure are designed by God to be between a man and a woman who are married.

The message of why his firing included public humiliation was more than personal. Time and again, conservative blacks who dare take on liberal conventions find themselves with their white counterparts, attacked and ostracized, threatened with unemployment and sometimes physical harm in an attempt to crush any notion that your religion has place in the public square.

Chief Cochran is yet another infuriating example where chains are put on any and all who dare to express anti-LWLP orthodoxy. The indivisible invisible who preach equality of income but not opportunity and tolerance of sin but not of righteousness have legions of followers scouring the internet seeking whom they may next devour.

Fall outside the rapidly changing gender-neutral orthodoxy and find yourself a pariah in need of a defensive tweet from Donald Trump.

WHERE NEXT

Implicit in President Ronald Reagan's observation when dealing with the issues of his day was that the key difference between America and the Soviet Union was God and truth. Communism is about power, politics, atheism, and materialism. Americanism is not.

The great and unique reality of America is that people don't get to just make up principles according to their whims or passions. That only happens in a society run by the politics of socialism or its hardcore bedmate, communism.

America was built on the premise that there are absolute truths and we receive them from above. To be an American is to try to live by them. Because they are universal and eternal principles, they are true for everyone and at all times.

Reagan knew that communism and its cousin socialism would fail because they are all about politics and political operatives determining how we live.

When Americans started taking God out of the equation, denigrating appreciation that there are immutable eternal truths according to which we must live, more and more started turning to government and politics to fix our lives—no different from the Soviet Union.

At that point, the connection between *E pluribus* and *unum* was broken.

We lost the eternal principles, true for all, that turn diversity into unity. And now diversity means lifestyle choices without barriers. And an aggressive youth movement to promote them.

The left has turned to politicians and our courts for the past fifty years to recreate our nation that has now become oppressive. Many American frogs leapt from a boiling pot.

The left wants to decide what the world is about, who we are, what we should do, what we should have, and how we should live. It sees any claim to faith and absolute truth as oppression.

But that's fake news. Truth actually enables diversity. Truth not only is the basis upon which we recognize the uniqueness of every individual, but it defines the barriers over mankind to help each unique individual self-govern.

God created a diverse world. He made man, and He made woman. And each man and each woman He made unique.

Each must play their own special role in the pursuit and implementation of the wisdom found in eternal truths that go way beyond any single individual. We are all unique and vital in discovering what is greater than us and beyond us. This is why the gender-neutral identity promoters must be challenged in the public square and public policy.

If there is nothing greater and beyond us, then we are not connected to eternity; thus, we are open to easy manipulation by materialism or plunder by politicians.

Once materialism or politicians start defining who we are and where we belong, we lose our uniqueness.

How can any politician be so pretentious to think they know who I am, what I want, and what I need just by knowing that I am a woman and that I am black?

How can any liberal driven by materialism or communism be so pretentious to think they know the motives, intents, or desires of my unique heart?

How can any politician or judge be so pretentious to think that they can legislate according to what a gay lobby deems good for each and every unique individual who is trying to process their sexual emotions?

Once appreciation of what the nation's founders knew—that freedom is about limited government and that limited government is only possible by knowing there is eternal truth from our Creator—is lost, government grows and politicians rule.

Once this appreciation is lost and sexual neutrality is enshrined into our national fabric, diversity becomes a political end rather than a vital condition for a free society.

The culture war continues, but now with a sleepless tweeter to wake us all up and perhaps keep us awake into and throughout his second term.

PART FOUR

BLACK NOISE

CHAPTER TEN

Goddess Oprah and Auntie Maxine

I N THE 1980s, way before the swipe-right culture of Tinder, *SJW* was a common abbreviation in newspaper personal ads for a single Jewish woman in search of a date.

Now, *SJW* stands for something much more dangerous—the Twitter social justice warrior of the perpetually offended who travels from alleged indiscretion to alleged indiscretion with their 140-character guillotines still bloody from the last life they destroyed. And they are using the tragedies in American black history to further their extreme cause.

No judge, no jury—just the Twitter mob arriving, attacking, destroying, and then moving to its next victims. The SJWs are the social media equivalent of Antifa, only they hide behind the anonymity of their computer keyboards rather than the skull-faced masks of the communist street fighters they so admire.

Internet anonymity provides them the perfect intimidation outlet to exact revenge, oftentimes disproportionate revenge to the alleged offense.

The concept of an "eye for an eye" from the Bible's Old Testament was seen in its time as a major shift in justice seeking, imposing the idea that the punishment must fit the crime.

The idea of fair justice that for now remains a centerpiece for our legal system is the presumption of innocence until proven guilty before a jury of your peers. Yet, in the street justice of the internet, guilt is presumed without jury so long as the accuser is part of the right hyphenated, protected class and the accused is not.

The indivisible invisible world of Twitter feeds off rage against those it calls white, male, Christian privileged unless, of course, you are a conservative, hyphenated other like Kelvin Cochran—then you're thrown into the privileged category, and its street justice will swiftly destroy any major player in any high-powered position.

There can be no room for diversity of thought and opinion within any gleaming buildings of capitalism, the elite halls of academia, union-controlled media, or elsewhere, including churches. The success of driving powerful men to capitulation has positioned mob rule to become the new and final ruling authority for standards of acceptable and unacceptable in America.

EXHIBIT A: BILL COSBY

"Hey, hey, hey. It's Fat Albert" is the way many Americans were introduced to Bill Cosby, a stand-up comedian who used his experiences growing up in Philadelphia to entertain audiences. Unlike Richard Pryor or even Red Foxx, Cosby's humor was family friendly and funny.

Some were introduced to Cosby and Robert Culp as a duo of hip spies in the television show *I Spy*, in which Cosby was the first black actor to play a lead role in a television drama.

But most people came to know him as the kindly, sweater-wearing father Cliff Huxtable, a doctor with an attorney wife living an upper-middle-class life raising successful kids in Brooklyn.

Cosby was so popular that he sold young people Jell-O Pudding Pops in television commercials that seemed omnipresent at the time.

Throughout the first four decades of Bill Cosby's career, he was the guy who everyone wanted to be friends with: funny, affable, and just a good guy.

And somehow this image persisted through almost fifty years of his career, even though sexual assault crimes exposed now date back to the late 1960s.

What changed to cause a dam of damnation to break against him and unveil his horrible crimes?

As early as 2004, Cosby began to speak out urging black parents to be more responsible for their children's development and telling black kids to "pull up their pants."

By 2009, Cosby was under attack for having the audacity to not solely blame racism for black people's struggles. Next, when he criticized President Obama's knee-jerk support for a Harvard professor who alleged police misconduct against a Cambridge police officer, it was on, with President Obama commenting on the rape allegations against Cosby in 2015.

Bill Cosby's apparent double life of being America's favorite dad during prime time and a serial rapist by late night had been covered up for years.

After his audacity to question a liberal tenet of faith—that racism is at the core of every black problem—his criminal past was uncovered.

The left cannot afford for the black community to walk away from providing it votes even as it continually betrays the community's interest through supporting open borders, opposing God, promoting infanticide and Planned Parenthood clinics in inner-city neighborhoods, and undermining economic and educational opportunities that threaten to break the shackles of government dependency.

Step outside of accepted, allowed speech or thought, and the keepers of keys to the chains and your personal secrets will seek to crush you.

EXHIBIT B: HARVEY WEINSTEIN

Harvey Weinstein did not invent the casting couch. Those with power in the entertainment industry, both male and female, heterosexual or not, have been abusing it since before Hollywood and Vine became famous.

One has to wonder what conservative thought he may have uttered to land in their crosshairs after decades of abusing women.

It is clear from the outside that Weinstein's abuses were both known and accepted as an almost Hollywood ritual for those young women hoping for a trip to the top. As Seth MacFarlane joked upon listing the nominees for best supporting actress, "Congratulations. You five ladies no longer have to pretend to be attracted to Harvey Weinstein."

Did the members of the glittering Oscar crowd rise up in revulsion? No, they laughed and, in 2013, ducked the obvious issue that had been raised.

But in 2017, Weinstein's world collapsed as the very culture that he had helped build turned on him. Dear friends like Oprah Winfrey suddenly found themselves caught in the SJW street justice spin cycle that threatened to undo careers, and Weinstein went from feared to ruined.

Eventually the accusations will come to trial, but the adjudication is over, and Weinstein is finished.

As for the long friendship Oprah had with Weinstein and Cosby?

She emerged unjudged and unscathed from the wrath of the SJWs.

Why?

Because Oprah is the goddess of the left.

Oprah Winfrey has become a modern-day pied piper for most divisions of race matters and sex matters in America combined.

But like most false prophets or goddesses, one day their fraud is exposed.

STORY OF THE PIED PIPER

The Pied Piper is a legendary character of a story from a small town in Germany called Hamelin. The legend dates back to the Middle Ages, with the earliest references describing a piper dressed in multicolored clothing hired by the town to lure rats away with his magic pipe. The politics of Oprah remind me of the story of the Pied Piper.

In one version of the Pied Piper story, the people of the town refuse to pay for him to rid the town of rats, so he retaliates by using his instrument's magical power on their children, leading them away as he had the rats. The other story of folklore is that the Pied Piper was simply a symbol of hope to the people of Hamelin, which had been attacked by plague, and he drove the rats away, saving the people from the epidemic.

I'm not actually saying that Oprah is a *rat catcher*, but her tactics of luring a vulnerable community of African Americans into ideas of secularism and socialism should not be left unchallenged. Whether she is just an angry, aging, unmarried woman in retaliation who, regardless of her bank account, is still of a historical people from Africa or whether she's driven by the reality that her celebrity world is nothing more than folklore beliefs, myths, and entertaining yet unrealistic tales of La La Land, Oprah demands that her followers come see the world as she does.

Today, the legend of Pied Piper has morphed into something negative, and three of its particulars could define the Oprah of today:

1. A person who offers other people strong and delusive enticements.
2. A vivacious leader who makes irresponsible and alluring promises.
3. A person who entices people to follow them in a particular course of action.

Oprah Winfrey had reached the pinnacle of the American dream: wealth, popularity, talent, and, most importantly, a personality that convinced everyone to assume that she understood their values, hopes, and dreams.

Then she got involved in politics. Then she turned her wrath against the very founding principles of America that elevated her name to becoming a household word. Then she turned rage on the very audience that made her rich and famous by diminishing her lofty persona to black victim.

"I'm in a store and the person doesn't obviously know that I carry the black card and so they make an assessment based upon the way I look and who I am," said Oprah to *Entertainment Tonight* the year after President Obama was reelected and she earned $77 million.

Yep, the $38,000 purse in Switzerland.

"I didn't have anything that said 'I have money': I wasn't wearing a diamond stud. I didn't have a pocketbook. I didn't wear Louboutin shoes. I didn't have anything," said the goddess.

"You should be able to go in a store looking like whatever you look like and say, 'I'd like to see this.' That didn't happen."

No, that is not true even for goddess Oprah. Shopkeepers actually have the right to post signs that say "no shirt, no shoes, no service." Restaurants have the right to say "no flip-flops or sneakers" and "men must wear a jacket." Lamborghini dealers do not have to turn over keys to their cars to anyone and everyone who walks onto their car lot. And it doesn't always mean racism.

It would have been okay that she was an Obama supporter; after all, the first black president was historic. Her fans voted for him, and as the beloved black icon of suburban women, the world was Oprah's oyster.

But the party ended when both she and Obama tried to convince the entire world that the burden of being black in America is so severe it needs to be mentioned over and over and over again. Day after day, week after week, month after month, year after year, for generations.

That no matter how rich or famous or presidential, at the end of the day, most white people could never be trusted to not wake up every morning without racism against all blacks on their minds.

Most American households barely clear forty grand in a year, especially the housewives who enjoyed her television show while their kiddies napped. These Americans had a hard time wrapping their minds around her accusations. How could she, whom they adored, think they were closeted racists?

How could she use something so petty as not being recognized in that store to declare that America had not matured from her horrific past of slavery and Jim Crow? What would redemption look like, and could it ever even occur? In that moment, Oprah had stolen their hope for the change President Obama had promised. Her very audience began to feel abandoned, hurt, and thrown under a racial rug, and, thus, they grew pretty frustrated.

Pied Oprah could have healed America's race war with her whimsical pipe had she wanted to and preserved her goddess image, but instead she went black noise.

Her shining stardom diminished yet another notch in their eyes when she embraced the far-left Black Lives Matter agenda, rejecting racial reconciliation in favor of a vengeful, hate-motivated agenda designed to end the rule of law in America.

By then her fans had had enough, and many now find a change agent in Donald Trump. The luster of Oprah tarnished a little more in the wake of #MeToo allegations that she introduced at least one young woman to Harvey Weinstein along with the pictures to prove it. All of her reputation as a goddess for good washed up.

She, along with Obama, could have been celebrated throughout history and forever lionized as great racial healers, written into the final legacy chapter of fulfilling Dr. King's incredible dream.

Instead, both Oprah and Obama succumbed; they are nothing more than rich and powerful black LWLPs. What a waste.

AUNTIE MAXINE

During the first year of the Obama administration, a colleague and I sat down for dinner in a popular Washington, D.C., restaurant.

As he looked over the menu, my colleague noticed President Obama's Health and Human Services secretary, Kathleen Sebelius, sitting at a nearby table. The presence and accessibility of Sebelius, very much the public face of the health care initiative that would become the Affordable Care Act—Obamacare—brought my usually sober, cerebral, conservative friend to tremors.

He, like conservatives across the nation, was livid at the intention of the Obama administration to bring health care, one-sixth of the national economy, under unprecedented government control. He told me he was going to go to her table and share with her a piece of his mind.

Fortunately, he got hold of himself and realized, as outraged as he was, that to approach the secretary at her dinner table was improper, and he backed off.

I think most Americans would agree that my colleague's decision, driven by his deep convictions, to take control of his passion was commendable and that he submitted that passion to the rules of civility and the decorum of proper public discourse.

Unfortunately, today, we are seeing an increasing number of our citizens failing the challenge of self-control and allowing themselves to cross the line of civility and interfering, sometimes violently, with the private lives of public officials, public spokespeople, or political figures.

When then–House Majority Whip Steve Scalise was shot by a gunman at a public park in Virginia where Republican congressmen were practicing for the annual Congressional Baseball Game for Charity, many of us inside the Beltway wondered aloud if America was on the verge of another civil war.

The attorney general of Virginia concluded that the gunman's motive was "rage against Republican legislators" and called this "an act of terrorism."

Peaceful public discourse and disagreement are the oxygen of a free and democratic society. There is no question that this becomes challenging at times like the present when our nation is so deeply divided. Given these challenges, it is particularly egregious when a member of Congress speaks out and encourages behavior disruptive to the peaceful and civil public discourse so essential to our society and urges private citizens to interfere with the ability of fellow Americans to live their private lives.

During the aftermath of the tragic attempted assassination of more than a dozen GOP House members as they practiced for a charity baseball game against their Democrat counterparts, a bipartisan group of forty-six House members signed a pledge of civility toward one another.

The pledge clearly stated:

> Although we represent both political parties and a wide range of individual views across the political spectrum, our common and sincere aims are to serve the needs and interests of the American people, to work with one another to encourage greater confidence in our institutions, and to set an example of statesmanship for the younger generations of Americans that will follow.
>
> To this end, we are dedicated to showing proper respect to one another and all others, encouraging productive dialogue, and modeling civility in our public and private actions. While we may vehemently disagree on matters of law and policy, we will strive at all times to maintain collegiality and the honor of our office.

Throughout Maxine Waters's political career, the hatred she has expressed against her opposition has been not benign but calculated. Calculated to always intimidate those who don't agree with her. But in early summer of 2018, after the aging LWLPs had watched her power unravel over eighteen months in which more and more blacks personally felt the positive impact of President Trump's agenda, Auntie Maxine, as her dearest supporters call her, had a meltdown unmatched by a candy-deprived two-year-old in a grocery store.

This is what we heard from Congresswoman Maxine Waters: "Let's make sure we show up wherever we have to show up," she told a crowd in Los Angeles. "And if you see anybody from that Cabinet in a restaurant, in a department store, at a gasoline station, you get out and create a crowd. And you push back on them. And you tell them they're not welcome anymore."

Senate and House Minority Leaders Chuck Schumer and Nancy Pelosi rebuked Waters for these irresponsible remarks. House Speaker Paul Ryan asked Waters to apologize, but she refused.

The House should have voted to censure Congresswoman Waters as a statement that "we the people" will not tolerate such behavior by our elected representatives.

The Constitution authorizes the House to discipline and punish members for "disorderly behavior," according to the Congressional Research Service, "to protect the institutional integrity of the House of Representatives, its proceedings, and its reputation."

It is profoundly damaging to the institutional integrity of the House when one of its members urges private citizens to disrupt the private lives of public officials and "push back on them."

The job of members of Congress is to enlighten and represent citizens, not incite them to disruptive behavior. This pathetic moment in our country required a full and complete repudiation of her words using the House censure process before the inevitable occurs.

The litany of attacks and confrontations of Trump supporters and officials have only grown larger and more outrageous since even before the 2016 election, and the public emboldening of physical and psychological bullying is dangerous for our nation's future.

It is tragic when deranged people like the Congressional baseball field shooter move from Bernie Sanders activist to assassin, but when violence is encouraged by a member of Congress, it is no longer an isolated incident but an orchestrated assault on our political system and basic freedoms.

Our nation is strong enough to survive the honest debate of competing ideas; what our nation cannot survive is when one side, the left, will no longer talk and is devolving into a violent mob.

Maxine Waters effectively yelled fire in a crowded theater, and it was up to then Speaker Paul Ryan and the rest of Congress to attempt to restore calm in our society as we work through the noisy divisions in America being exposed under President Trump.

Oh well. Their missed opportunity while President Trump expressed his leadership style once again with one simple tweet.

BLACK CONFORMITY SPLIT

The once-hidden agendas of LWLPs including captain Maxine Waters and once-poised Oprah Winfrey have become much more exposed by the emergence of new faces in the Democratic Party— more progressive, more left-wing faces—leaving a lot to explain to a major part of their loyalist base.

While the legacy of slavery and Jim Crow racism that followed have left a long and ugly imprint on our nation, the majority of African Americans today live comfortably in the middle class.

According to the U.S. Census Bureau, 87 percent of black adults have a high school diploma, 23 percent have a bachelor's degree, and almost half own their own home. From 2002 to 2007, the number of black-owned business increased by 60.5 percent to 1.9 million, more than triple the national rate of 18.0 percent.

So why do black leaders like Oprah and Auntie Maxine keep carrying the water of the left, throwing salt on the healing wound to replay America's past and see only political solutions to moral problems of those trapped in poverty or broken black neighborhoods?

Dr. Martin Luther King Jr. was right to see the racial dilemma of our nation as a moral dilemma and define the civil rights movement that he led as a moral, Christian-driven movement. He insisted that his organization be called the Southern Christian Leadership Conference.

His famous "I Have a Dream Speech" was a sermon by a Christian pastor. It wasn't a political speech. "Now is the time to make justice a reality for all of God's children," he said as he quoted many prophets of the Bible.

I think far too many black LWLP leaders like Oprah and the congresswoman have deep disdain for the fact that the civil rights movement in its entirety was animated by the imagery and the language of the Bible.

Disdain so deep that after all was said and done, Dr. King's movement and its great achievements in the Civil Rights Act of 1964 and Voting Rights Act of 1965 have degenerated into the politics of victimization.

When the job was to call the entire nation to task so that all Americans receive equal treatment under the law, that the great truths embedded in our Declaration of Independence and Constitution be applied equally to all Americans, the Civil Rights Act and Voting Rights Act could have culminated into the part of Dr. King's admonition that we go back to our communities and build.

Instead, the left expanded government into special interest groups and diversity groups that do nothing more than lobby for secularism and statism. It is these efforts that opened the door for new tensions in the public square that have escalated into our current culture war.

It was here that America saw the birth of political correctness and identity politics.

Once the sins of slavery and racism were no longer seen as a sins but a political problem, black interests were transformed into a generic political issue tied to ethnicity with political solutions rather than a moral issue requiring moral restitution.

African Americans became the pawns in the LWLP chess game against America's founding principles of Christianity, capitalism, and our Constitution.

But now, the political party that sold this message and demanded conformity from all blacks is delivering more candidates around the nation who are unabashedly boilerplate, in-your-face, hard left. Pro–big government, pro-abortion, pro-LGBTQ rights.

But African Americans generally don't fit the new far-left profile.

According to recent data from the Pew Research Center, black Democrats have very little religiously in common with white Democrats. Religious behavior of black Democrats is much more closely aligned with white Republicans.

Forty-seven percent of black Democrats say they attend church at least weekly compared with 45 percent of white Republicans and 22 percent of white Democrats.

Ninety-two percent of black Protestants say they believe in God as described in the Bible compared with 70 percent of Republicans and 45 percent of Democrats.

In the Pew Religious Landscape study published in 2014, 36 percent of historically black Protestants described themselves as conservative and 24 percent as liberal.

Regarding the role of government, 23 percent of historically black Protestants say they prefer smaller government and fewer services, and 70 percent say they prefer larger government and more services.

Regarding government aid to the poor, 27 percent of historically black Protestants say government does more harm than good, and 66 percent say government does more good than harm.

The data reported above are for what Pew defines as "historically black Protestants," which, according to Pew, consist of 53 percent of all blacks. However, according to Pew, 79 percent of blacks identify as Christian. Pew reports that in addition to 47 percent of all black Democrats saying they attend church at least once per week, 74 percent say they pray daily, and 76 percent say religion is "very important" in their lives. So, data that Pew reports for historically black Protestants seem to be a reasonably rough sample of black attitudes in general. When 36 percent of blacks identify as conservative and when 27 percent say government assistance to the poor does more harm than good yet on average 88 percent of blacks are voting for Democrats, something is amiss.

Voting Democratic is not written in black genes. From 1936 to 1960, the black vote for the Republican presidential candidate averaged 30 percent. In 1956, 39 percent of blacks voted for Dwight Eisenhower. Black voting behavior has far-reaching implications, as America changes demographically into a country less and less white. In 1980, 88 percent of voters were white. In 2016, 70 percent were. This trend will continue.

In a recent Harvard-Harris Poll, 33 percent of blacks say they are now "better off" in their financial situation and 32 percent of blacks approve of the way Trump is handling the economy.

Republican Party outreach to blacks has ratcheted up considerably since the Obama years. If Republicans succeed in courting church-going black Christians, we could see a political realignment in the country that will profoundly change America's political landscape.

Not good news for the left. News that perhaps is another reason LWLP members Oprah and Auntie have gone absolutely anti-Trump mad.

CHAPTER ELEVEN

No Police, No Peace

A MERICA WAS founded on the idea that individual rights come from God and they are not bestowed by the government.

This idea is translated into America's governance document, the Constitution, through the precept that the laws are created through the consent of the governed and as such must be enforced until those elected officials change them.

Part of the genius of the United States is that power is dispersed to state and local governments rather than being held tightly in Washington, D.C., and policing is one area where federalism is most important.

Rather than depend upon an omnipresent national police force, the power of policing is largely held by state and local governments.

While this dispersal of police power has inherent downsides in that departments can become parochial and serving of the local elite to the detriment of the rest of the citizenry, by and large the idea of the police officer who arrives at your door being a neighbor or even friend makes for better law enforcement. Some of the questions of police brutality today have more to do with unionization of civil servants and conditions of family life for young men post–Jim Crow, which I will address in a bit.

But the Obama administration's Justice Department's Office on

Civil Rights engaged in a comprehensive campaign to change local policing and end effective crime control measures like former New York City Mayor Rudy Giuliani's successful yet controversial broken windows policy.

The concept of broken windows, which worked in New York City and in other cities like Baltimore, Maryland, under former Mayor Martin O'Malley, was for police to aggressively interdict crime through enforcing loitering laws and pursuing other petty crimes. This policy significantly reduced every level of crime including homicides, but the cost was that blacks, particularly unmarried young black men, were saddled with arrest records that became barriers to employment and full integration into the economy.

Into this challenge, the Obama administration working with the George Soros backed Black Lives Matter ($33 million), and Soros's allies in the Democracy Alliance pledged another $100 million with the goal of sowing discord against the police, undermining the legitimacy of the rule of law itself by attacking the enforcers of the law.

Aggressively using social media and a highly sophisticated left-wing communications network, Black Lives Matter became adept at the latest social media trend of driving legitimate concerns about unequal treatment under the law into full-fledged rioting in response to police self-defense shootings.

The truth is that there are some bad police shootings and there are some corrupt and/or racist cops. But the Black Lives Matter movement makes no attempt to distinguish between good and bad, automatically declaring that the police were always at fault and that America's system of laws was determined to be racist at its core.

HANDS UP, DON'T SHOOT

Of course, the results of a "the police are guilty-no-matter-the-facts" radicalism is that cops began to withdraw from areas that are primarily black or Hispanic for self-protection. Police morale and recruitment suffered as the slogan "Hands up, don't shoot" took hold in every crime-ridden, distressed community across America after the Ferguson, Missouri, police shooting death of Michael Brown went viral on the internet in 2014.

The shooting of Michael Brown occurred on August 9, 2014, in Ferguson, Missouri, a northern suburb of St. Louis. Brown, an eighteen-year-old African American walking with a friend in the center of a two-way road, was fatally shot by Darren Wilson, a twenty-eight-year-old white police officer. Wilson said that an altercation ensued when Brown attacked Wilson in his police vehicle for control of Wilson's gun until it was fired. Brown and his friend then fled, with Wilson in pursuit of Brown.

Wilson stated that Brown stopped and charged him after a short pursuit. In the entire altercation, Wilson fired a total of twelve bullets, including two during the struggle in the car. Brown was hit a total of six times from the front, the last probably the fatal shot.

This event ignited unrest in Ferguson.

Although a subsequent FBI investigation found that there was no evidence that Brown had his hands up in surrender or said "don't shoot" before he was shot, protesters believed that he had and used the slogan "Hands up, don't shoot" in protest. Protests, both peaceful and violent, continued for more than a week in Ferguson; police established a nightly curfew.

The response of area police agencies in dealing with the protests was strongly criticized by the media and politicians. There were concerns over insensitivity, tactics, and a militarized response. Missouri Governor Jay Nixon ordered local police organizations to cede much of their authority to the Missouri State Highway Patrol.

A grand jury was called, was given extensive evidence, and decided not to indict Wilson. The U.S. Department of Justice was called in to investigate and cleared Wilson of civil rights violations in the shooting.

It found that forensic evidence supported the officer's account, that witnesses who corroborated the officer's account were credible, and that witnesses who had incriminated him were not credible, with some admitting they had not directly seen the events.

The U.S. Department of Justice issued a report on the shooting that said, "There is no witness who has stated that Brown had his hands up in surrender whose statement is otherwise consistent with the physical evidence" and "our investigation did not reveal any eyewitness who stated that Brown said 'don't shoot.'"

The U.S. Department of Justice concluded that Officer Darren Wilson had shot Michael Brown in self-defense.

HANDS OFF, HANDS UP

"Hands up, don't shoot," or simply "hands up," is a slogan and gesture originating from the incident and was seen in demonstrations in Ferguson and throughout the United States. The gesture became a rallying cry against police violence. Only it was a fabrication of imagination. A campaign slogan of sorts rooted in the agenda of activist George Soros to undermine law and order in America.

Michael Brown did not have his hands up according to many who were there that tragic night. But the intimidation mob insisted on a hands-off approach regarding the truth.

Numerous witness accounts were consistent with Wilson's account and also agreed with the physical evidence at hand. Many witnesses confirmed that Wilson had acted in self-defense during the event. A number of the witnesses who corroborated Wilson's account of events expressed fear and apprehension in testifying, saying they had been harassed or threatened by individuals from the Ferguson community.

Following are samples of witness accounts aligned with Wilson's testimony.

Witness 102 was a twenty-seven-year-old biracial male. He said he saw Wilson chase Brown until Brown abruptly turned around. Brown did not put his hands up in surrender but made some type of movement similar to pulling his pants up or a shoulder shrug and then made a full charge at Wilson. Witness 102 thought Wilson's life was threatened and he only fired shots when Brown was coming toward him.

Witness 103, a fifty-eight-year-old black male, testified that from his parked truck he saw "Brown punching Wilson at least three times in the facial area, through the open driver's window of the SUV. Wilson and Brown [had] hold of each other's shirts, but Brown was 'getting in a couple of blows [on Wilson].'"

Witness 104, a twenty-six-year-old biracial female, witnessed the end of the altercation from a minivan and said she saw Brown run from the SUV, followed by Wilson, who "hopped" out of the SUV and ran after him while yelling "stop, stop, stop." Wilson did not fire his gun as Brown ran from him. Brown then turned around and "for a second" began to raise his hands as though he may have considered surrendering but then quickly "balled up in fists" in a running position and "charged" at Wilson. Witness 104 explained that it took some time for Wilson to fire, adding that she "would have fired sooner."

Witness 108, a seventy-four-year-old black male, told detectives that the police officer was "in the right" and "did what he had to do" and that statements made by people in the apartment complex about Brown surrendering were inaccurate. Witness 108 later told investigators he "would have f-ing shot that boy, too" and mimicked the aggressive stance Brown made while charging Wilson. He explained that Wilson told Brown to "stop" or "get down" at least ten times but instead Brown "charged" at Wilson. Witness 108 also told detectives that there were other witnesses on Canfield Drive who saw what he did.

Witness 109, a fifty-three-year-old black male, said he decided to come forward after seeing Dorian Johnson "lie" about the events on television. He said when Wilson asked the two boys to get out of the street, Brown responded something to the effect of "F—k the police." Afterward, Wilson got out of his car and Brown hit him in the face. Witness 109 said he saw Wilson reach for his Taser but dropped it and then grabbed a gun, after which Brown grabbed for Wilson's gun. According to 109, at one point, Brown ran away from Wilson, but he turned around and charged toward the officer. He said Wilson fired in self-defense and did not appear to be shooting to kill at first.

Witness 113, a thirty-one-year-old black female, made statements that corroborated Wilson's account. She said she was afraid of the "neighborhood backlash" that might come from her testimony and feared offering an account contrary to the narrative reported by the media that Brown held his hands up in surrender. She also told investigators she thought Wilson's life was in danger.

GOOD MORNING, BALTIMORE

The net effect of impoverished communities run by local gangs and drive-by mobs, leaving the residents subject to the whims of the street rather than the protections afforded by the law, is yet another reason 1.2 million African Americans voted for Donald Trump in 2016. He did ask them during his campaign, "What do you have to lose?" Many of these black voters knew that their very lives were at stake.

If the new norm after every local police incident was Al Sharpton and BLM showing up with prepackaged slogans, signs, and paid protesters, this wasn't going to work for all blacks, especially not for those raising boys in our nation's most crime-flush zip codes.

Not surprisingly, homicide rates in places like Baltimore, Maryland, skyrocketed as a direct result of the hands-off policing policy that came directly from Black Lives Matter.

And who does the majority of dying in the resulting new homicide wave? That's right, blacks.

In the Charm City, home of the Orioles and Ravens, the homicide crisis can be directly correlated to the death of a local drug dealer— Freddie Gray—and the trials of six police officers (three white men, two black men, and a black woman) on various charges related to his death. Of those who went to trial, all were either acquitted or had the charges dropped by the prosecution.

But the prosecution changed Baltimore policing. Criminology professor and former police officer Anthony Jay Mosko observed in a *USA Today* interview, "Cops are doing as requested, lessening racial disparity, lessening complaints, lessening police involved shootings.

All those numbers are just great right now, and if those are your metrics for success, we're winning."

The article doesn't reflect whether Mosko was being facetious or serious, but Black Lives Matter making the police the bad guys when taking drug dealers off the streets and interdicting small crimes before they become big ones has produced predictable results. Crime and homicide rates went through the roof post–Freddie Gray police sensitivity training, and in 2015 Baltimore hit its highest per capita homicide rate in history.

Black Lives Matters's Baltimore legacy is that black lives are being lost at a higher rate than ever before as its war on cops has disastrous consequences for the vast majority of law-abiding citizens. And incredibly the same horrific story is being played out in city after city around the nation, where the police are being told both directly and indirectly to stay out of the carnage communities unless they are called and stand down when they are.

Beyond the increased tensions between the police serving and people living in our nation's distressed zip codes directly attributable to Black Lives Matter, it is the rule of law that is most damaged. When people are afraid of the law enforcers, the violence is really against our Constitution itself. Given that our laws are directly from those who are elected by the people, the entire American system of government by the consent of the governed is under assault. After self-defense options, the police are the next line of defense, and Black Lives Matter is intent on stripping both this and the self-protection line of defense away. Putting black lives needlessly at risk due to Black Lives Matters's assault on the rule of law and the enforcers of it is a national shame.

The primary funder of Black Lives Matters, George Soros, is only good for a selective few liberal black lives. All you have to do is follow the billions he gives to hard-core left-wing causes and you will find a real enemy of free blacks and especially free Christian blacks. Soros started the Open Society Institute in 1993 as a way to spread his wealth to LWLP causes and, using Open Society as a conduit, has given more than $7 billion to a who's who of destructive groups including National Council of La Raza, Tides Foundation, *Huffington Post*, Southern Poverty Law Center, Sojourners, People for the American Way, Planned Parenthood, and the National Organization for Women. The fact that Soros and his minions are putting black lives on their altar in order to tear apart the United States is a de facto war on America with poor vulnerable victims being their acceptable cost.

BROKEN WINDOWS, SAFE SIDEWALKS

The tragedy of Michael Brown is too common a story. As the human spirit of black youth across our country is suffocated under horrible circumstances of poverty, frustrations boil over and wind up in violent encounters, often with the police, and a young black man winds up pointlessly dead.

Wealthy black liberals, despite being living proof that the American dream works, who build businesses fueled by American capitalism, invariably join the ongoing chorus of the same failed explanations of why these impoverished communities persist generations after the Civil Rights Act became law.

Liberal black media serve up the same monotone left-wing propaganda and double-dare any black who objects to survive their venom. Nastier than a slithering snake, the costs for conservative blacks could be both professional and social suicide.

I broke out of the LWLP chains years ago, after seeing what the debilitating culture of the welfare state was doing to me and those around me, and although I was a little bruised, I survived their bunk and lived to write about it.

I started my own policy organization to provide research and information and forums for discussion to shed light on how the misguided government policies of the left keep the poor desperate rather than leading them out of the morass but also to point to good public policy like broken windows policing.

Crime is one major reason that poverty is entrenched in America's most distressed communities, and with a lack of good policing policy, crime will persist.

While the nation debated police policy during the Obama years, the policy of broken windows was taken to the woodshed for a beating. In the same way that every time there is gun violence at a school the gun is to blame, every time a local white cop shoots a suspected black criminal this policy is to blame.

The broken windows policy is the result of a criminological theory that visible signs of crime, anti-social behavior, and civil disorder create an urban environment that encourages further crime and disorder, including serious crimes. The theory suggests that policing methods that target minor crimes such as vandalism, public drinking, loitering, and fare evasion help to create an atmosphere of order and lawfulness, thereby preventing more serious crimes. We see this type of policing style in small towns and suburban communities all the time, but the theory headlined when urban mayors adopted the methods to bring discipline to large cities.

The broken windows theory was first introduced by social scientists James Q. Wilson and George L. Kelling in an article in the March 1982 edition of *The Atlantic Monthly*.

It garnered national attention in the 1990s when then New York City police commissioner William Bratton and Mayor Rudy Giuliani incorporated aspects of the idea in their NYC policing policies. The crack epidemic had just started, and urban communities were like war zones.

Under the broken windows theory, an ordered and clean environment, one that is maintained, sends the signal that the area is monitored and that criminal behavior is not tolerated. Conversely, a disordered environment of broken windows, graffiti, excessive litter, and loitering sends the signal that the area is not monitored and that criminal behavior has little risk of detection.

Full disclosure: I love the late James Quinn Wilson. Never met him, but he's alive on my phone in iBooks. My favorite book to reread over and over is *The Moral Sense*; I'm actually on page 413 of it again right now, and every sentence is again, right now, insightfully new wisdom.

When a neighborhood allows a building with a few broken windows to go unrepaired, it attracts vandals to break a few more windows or even break into the building. If that same neighborhood then allows an unoccupied building to stay unoccupied and unrepaired, either vandals or squatters will use that building, which could result in further damage or perhaps a fire. The concept of broken windows also addresses litter; if a neighborhood allows litter to accumulate on the pavement, then soon more litter accumulates. Soon people start to leave bags of refuse from local takeout restaurants and eventually break into cars.

James Q. Wilson and George L. Kelling received a great deal of attention and were very widely cited, which led to a 1996 criminology and urban sociology book called *Fixing Broken Windows: Restoring Order and Reducing Crime in Our Communities,* by George L. Kelling and Catharine Coles, a book with dog-eared pages for many working in Washington on welfare reform during the 1990s. Wilson, Kelling, and Coles were major thought leaders on crime at that time. Kelling and Coles argued in their book that a successful strategy for preventing vandalism is to address the problems when they are small. Repair the broken windows within a short time—say, a day or a week—and the tendency is that vandals are much less likely to break more windows or do further damage. Clean up the sidewalk every day, and the tendency is for litter not to accumulate.

Others chimed in that the presence of police authority is not enough to maintain safe sidewalks. That broken windows and vandalism are prevalent because the residents simply do not care about the damage. That residents of neighborhoods help with crime prevention. That people care for and protect what they have invested in.

Dare I say that marriage breakdown equals broken family equals broken windows? That safe sidewalks are in neighborhoods with men married to the mother of their children, men with respect for the police and the skill set to fix broken windows? Heresy and antithesis of LWLP philosophy.

CHAPTER TWELVE

Not All Blacks Allowed

A 2018 QUINNIPIAC University poll showed yet another perspective on the deep racial division in our country. Ninety-one percent of Democrats compared with 12 percent of Republicans agree with the statement that President Trump is racially biased against people of color. Looks more like what we call a racial divide today is really a partisan divide.

Consider the remarks of Rep. John Lewis, who decided not to attend the opening of the new Civil Rights Museum in Mississippi in 2017 because Trump announced he would attend. Lewis called Trump's attendance "an affront to the veterans of the civil rights movement."

Or look to the fact that the president of the NAACP also announced he would not attend because of Trump's presence. NAACP President Derrick Johnson called Trump's attendance at the museum's opening "a distraction from us having the opportunity to honor true Americans who sacrificed so much to ensure that democracy works."

The real affront or distraction to civil rights comes today from these left-wing black leaders who claim to represent the civil rights movement—some of whom actually fought in the 1960s for civil rights and fought for freedom against stereotyping any individual because of their race.

Freedom supposedly means living and thinking freely according to one's judgment and conscience; free blacks should be allowed to have conservative views as well as liberal views.

In 2016, 8 percent of black voters, or 1.2 million people, voted for Donald Trump. But these 1.2 million blacks don't have value according to mainstream blacks in politics, media, academia, or business.

Like the Dred Scott decision in 1857, which declared blacks inhuman and therefore not eligible to be American citizens, both black and white LWLPs have declared the same for black Republicans and black conservatives—and now black orthodox Christians.

About 15 percent of black men between the ages of eighteen and fifty-four voted for Donald Trump. By the summer of 2018, Trump's approval ratings reached 20 percent with black men and 15 percent with black women. Perhaps most African Americans aren't monolithic lock-stepped liberals after all, don't appreciate forced conformity, and need more than sanctimonious indignation from yesterday's civil rights leaders.

An honest black leader whose primary interest is black freedom and healing black communities, rather than left-wing politics, would be asking why so many black Americans voted for Donald Trump.

Instead, this question has begun to shake the left to its core as record numbers of twenty-first-century new black leaders and young voters have separated themselves from the pack to pursue new answers to old problems.

The problems in poor black communities today are solvable, and President Trump is determined to help solve them. Immediately upon starting his presidency, he began to implement the urban initiative to fix the inner cities that he spoke about on his campaign trail. First, he signed into law a capital gains tax incentive authored by Senators Tim Scott and Cory Booker and hidden deep inside the Tax Cuts and Jobs Act of 2017 that focused specifically on our nation's 8,700 distressed zip codes. His Treasury Department completed the regulations for this capital gains tax deferment in October 2018. President Trump then signed several executive orders to address many of the concerns of the people living in these zip codes, from streamlining existing anti-poverty programs in each federal department to setting up a special White House Council composed of top leaders to focus boots-on-the-ground energy within these zip codes.

It shouldn't be with great personal peril to anyone's reputation and social standing to support the Trump administration in exploring some possible new ideas. With such a heavy emphasis by our new president to fix what has broken down for our nation's citizens dwelling in our most distressed zip codes, there is a major opportunity at hand to help him get this done. Thus, many brave young blacks and members of the clergy are weathering the personal storm of SJW, Antifa, and the black left mob's harassment to seek fresh thought.

It's not a secret that having large communities of government-dependent poor people concentrated in government-run housing projects and union-controlled schools is a recipe for despair and disaster, mayhem, and murder. But this environment for three generations is okay for the local elected officials and congressional leaders of these zip codes. In fact, all forty-nine members of the Congressional Black Caucus will fight tooth and nail to keep these communities in chaos and keep the people living in them trapped in them.

Trump Inaugural Address, 2017

Americans want great schools for their children, safe neighborhoods for their families, and good jobs for themselves. These are the just and reasonable demands of a righteous public. But for too many of our citizens, a different reality exists: Mothers and children trapped in poverty in our inner cities; rusted-out factories scattered like tombstones across the landscape of our nation; an education system, flush with cash, but which leaves our young and beautiful students deprived of knowledge; and the crime and gangs and drugs that have stolen too many lives and robbed our country of so much unrealized potential. This American carnage stops right here and stops right now.

CBC January 19, 2017, Letter to DJT

Dear Mr. President-elect,

During your campaign, you pledged to address a number of issues being faced by African-Americans. Unfortunately, your "New Deal for Black America" represents the same old "Trickle Down" economics assumptions that didn't work for our communities in the 1980's or in the 2000's when these failed experiments were tried before.

Furthermore, your insistence on reducing the African-American experience solely to the conditions faced by many in our inner cities is ultimately unproductive. Thirty-nine percent of African-Americans live in suburbs compared to 36 percent who live in inner cities.

The remaining 25 percent live in small metropolitan areas and rural communities. For more than forty-five years, the Congressional Black Caucus (CBC) has worked to improve conditions for African-Americans from all walks of life. Collectively, our Members represent 78 million Americans, 17 million of whom are African-American. Our districts are rural as well as urban.

Some of our Members represent majority-minority districts while others do not. If you are serious about addressing issues in the African-American community, you would be wise to tap into the decades of expertise held by Members of our Caucus.

The CBC letter proceeded to pull apart point by point each idea of a ten-point document the Trump campaign released regarding fixing our inner cities called Trump's "New Deal for Black America with a Plan for Urban Renewal."[17]

What was number one of Trump's plan? "Great Education through School Choice."

We will allow every disadvantaged child in America to attend the public, private, charter, magnet, religious or home school of their choice. School choice is the great civil rights issue of our time, and

Donald Trump will be the nation's biggest cheerleader for school choice in all 50 states.

We will also ensure funding for Historic Black Colleges and Universities, more affordable 2 and 4-year college, and support for trade and vocational education.

It takes a lot of courage for a president to target almost a quarter of the federal budget for reform in an election year. But this is exactly what President Trump did with his April 2018 executive order "Reducing Poverty in America by Promoting Opportunity and Economic Mobility." We're now spending more than $700 billion per year on low-income assistance, which is more than we are spending on our national defense. And there are plenty of reasons to believe this spending is inefficient, wasteful, and counterproductive.

Over the past half century, some $22 trillion has been spent on anti-poverty programs, and yet the percentage of poor in this nation remains unchanged. And not only is it a matter of the percentage staying the same; people and families who are born poor stay that way.

The Better Way report produced by the House speaker's office in 2016 reported that 34 percent of those born and raised in the bottom fifth of the income scale remain there all their lives. The point has often been made that the greatest charitable gesture is teaching those in need to help themselves. This principle defines the president's reforms to our anti-poverty programs and spending. Let's make sure that every dollar spent goes to those truly in need and that those dollars are spent to maximize the likelihood that the recipients will get on their feet and become independent, productive, income-earning citizens.

The executive order directs federal agencies to review the eighty-plus federal anti-poverty programs, consolidate where there is redundancy and overlap, and look to reform by applying the principles of hard work and self-sufficiency.

Needless to say, the usual left-wing megaphones, those that can't tell the difference between compassion and spending billions of other people's dollars, wasted no time in going on the attack.

The headline from the Southern Poverty Law Center screams, "Trump's executive order on work requirements punishes low-income people for being poor."

Calling the executive order "heartless," the SPLC rejects the premise that there are those receiving benefits from these programs who could work but don't.

However, Robert Doar of the American Enterprise Institute reports that there are almost 20 million working-age Americans receiving benefits under Medicaid and food stamps who don't work.

The Better Way report notes that "44 percent of work-capable households using federal rental assistance report no annual income from wages."

But it's not just about work requirements.

Vital to this reform project is moving programs out of Washington's grasp and into the administrations at the state and local levels.

Assistance programs need humanity and flexibility. This can only be done locally. There's no way an army of bureaucrats in Washington can develop and implement programs for 50 million needy individuals and can properly recognize what unique individuals need to move out of poverty.

Assistance programs need to promote and embody those principles that go hand in hand with prosperity—ownership, investment, savings, and personal freedom and responsibility.

According to the Better Way report, almost 10 million Americans have no bank account and another 25 million have an account but get financial services outside the banking system.

When I was a young woman on welfare, I saw the destruction that occurs when assistance programs penalize work, marriage, and saving, as was the case with the Aid to Families with Dependent Children program.

Subsequently, this was reformed and transformed with great success to the Temporary Assistance for Needy Families program.

We can't go on spending hundreds of billions of dollars of limited taxpayer funds on programs that may have been conceived with sincerity and compassion but don't work.

President Trump deserves credit for exercising the courage and vision to move to fix what is broken in our anti-poverty programs. It is vital for the poor and vital for the nation.

CBC REBUTTAL TO NUMBER ONE ON TRUMP'S PLAN

Conversations around education reform and "school choice" often ignore the conditions outside the classroom that contribute to a student's performance. It is not enough to adjust a curriculum if we do not also address student hunger and account for parents having to work two or three jobs simply to make ends meet.

Rather than address these interconnected barriers to academic achievement, your plan would strip away $20 billion in funding from public schools in order to create the largest private school voucher program in American history.

The CBC supports access to good schools in all forms. However, simply shifting students from public to private schools does not ensure a quality education. A study into academic achievement of students in the Louisiana Scholarship Program, the largest existing voucher program, found a significant negative impact of voucher participation for math, reading, science, and social studies scores.

Voucher programs in Milwaukee, Cleveland and Washington, D.C., have not resulted in any significant score difference between voucher and non-voucher students.

Rather than diverting resources away from already under-resourced schools in pursuit of failed policies, the CBC would urge you to support methods that have been proven effective.

Furthermore, HBCUs play an indispensable role in training African-American professionals that work, live, and serve in communities across the nation. These institutions are indispensable to our communities, and it is not enough to simply promise to "ensure funding."

You must back up that promise by providing HBCUs the support and resources necessary to carry out their critical mission. If you want to make real progress towards improving educational

outcomes for African-Americans, you should embrace the policies
laid out by Ranking Member Bobby Scott in the Opening Doors for
Youth Act of 2016 and Rep. Marcia Fudge in the Core Opportunity
Resources for Equity and Excellence Act of 2015.

Five pages of rebuttal and regurgitation of the same stuff they've
been saying for fifty years, which hopefully is on the internet as I certainly don't want to have you fall asleep here.

My point bringing this up is twofold: first, I want to expose the
fact that members of the CBC are just a bunch of left-wing whiners of
the LWLPs. Their opening statement revealed no care for the problem
Trump set out to tackle: fixing the inner cities, places in serious distress.

Not problems of suburban blacks or rich blacks or healthy blacks.
Black people in need. Not the ninety-nine who were fine but the lost
sheep.

Eighty-five percent of black parents of children trapped in broken public schools support the voucher system that the CBC so adamantly disdains, and all of the voucher programs they attacked in
their rebuke have long waiting lists of desperate poor black parents.

And second, I want to show that the CBC has been reduced to an
overseer role. The day after the inauguration of Donald John Trump,
it slammed the door on any and all attempts to work with him, and
it guards that door against any African American who may want to
enter.

Its sole job during his presidency is to make sure any and all blacks
who attempt to work with DJT are made public examples: not one
shall escape the control of Democrats.

I expect we will see a lot more terror from Auntie Maxine and her
CBC colleagues as black support numbers are rising daily in support
of Trump serving a second term.

Oh, and by the way, one of DJT's early actions in the first month
of his presidency was in response to the CBC demand "You must
back up that promise by providing HBCUs the support and resources
necessary to carry out their critical mission."

The outcome? A delegation of presidents of historically black colleges and universities (HBCUs) was mocked, ridiculed, and scorned by the black left, the black overseers, and the entire SJW choir of LWLPs. Those HBCU presidents spent the rest of 2017 Black History Month in a long vicious media cycle explaining the photo taken of them by White House advisor Kellyanne Conway from a couch.

NOT A NEW DIVIDE

That blacks throughout U.S. history have been monolithic is a myth. Human nature attests to this fact. We are each uniquely made. But community—sticking together against bigger forces—is in African American DNA.

Some would argue that ideas of collectivism grew from tribal life in Africa where one's village was their community. It's one reason all Mom's friends are "Auntie" and the neighborhood youth are all "Cuz." Extended family collectivism was reality throughout slavery as every slave had each other's back and stepped up to take care of the kids, especially when a parent was sold off.

After slavery, the *I got your back* philosophy continued as 4 million former slaves adjusted to the reality of personal freedom in a demolished country torn in half by civil war. Kind of like how in an abusive marriage, once the fight is over and the TV is smashed, the kids help clean up the mess.

Adopting ideas of rugged individualism was a perilous option for blacks with Jim Crow, the Ku Klux Klan, and unions lurking behind every move. And although history has recorded variations in black next-move discussions from Marcus Garvey to Claude McKay to communist black organizations such as the African Blood Brotherhood (ABB), it was in the activities of the unions that black unity started to fracture back into tribes.

While unions were in lockstep to keep black former slaves from integrating workplaces and housing, many unions of the forties were communist- or socialist-led, so they developed black outreach programs to expand their driving philosophy that capitalism was evil and represented colonialism.

Prominent blacks throughout the twentieth century attracted to philosophies of Marxism, Leninism, and Stalinism include William Lorenzo Patterson, Asa Philip Randolph, Paul Robeson, Langston Hughes, Richard Wright, Ralph Ellison, Lena Horne, Dick Gregory, Sidney Poitier, Danny Glover, and Angela Davis, just to name a few to point out deviations from collectivism and monolithic demands throughout black American history.

And what has happened that these debates and deviations of black thoughts are not allowed?

Who decided that there would be a narrative to control all black sentiment regarding philosophy, politics, the pulpit, and the public square in the twenty-first century?

On July 1, 1991, Justice Clarence Thomas was confirmed to the U.S. Supreme Court. Because President George H. W. Bush nominated him, the left began a white-hot assault against him because he was not the right kind of black person. Yes, his skin color met the test, but his philosophy was troubling.

Venom that he was not authentically black became the mantra from every special interest group in the LWLP movement.

This *destroy your opponent* strategy persisted through the twentieth century and has grown into what Justice Thomas prophetically called a high-tech lynching. Back then there was no internet for the LWLPs, SJWs, and Antifa and their high-tech black overseers to abuse.

Today, even a hint that one has strayed from the ascribed groupthink for black people begins an investigation into whether a person is black enough, continues over the social media coals of public opinion to mark one as *traitor*, and ends with death threats.

The list of black traitors, Uncle Toms, and Aunt Jemimahs is getting so long that soon black conservatives will be the majority voice of African Americans.

More proof of left-wing terror tactics occurred in summer 2018 when a prominent group of black pastors met with President Trump to discuss prison reform. These members of the clergy, as with all blacks in association with the Trump administration, had to withstand a withering assault from the left.

Prison reform is a real issue that affects blacks disproportionately and that the Trump administration had been working on since his first day in the Oval Office under the leadership of his son-in-law Jared Kushner. The prison reform initiative had already passed the House and was lagging in the Senate, so this meeting was called.

Immediately the indivisible invisible SJWs hit the World Wide Web. Pastor Van Moody of Birmingham had to defend his attendance at the White House. Pastor John Gray said what Jesse Jackson used to say: that we can't influence policy if we are not seated at the table.

Their attendance was an important and commendable step for black conservatives. One-third of African Americans poll on the side of pursuing truth, and the more public voices they have, the more secure they are to live as free people.

It's incredible that a meeting to discuss the overincarceration of black people between members of the clergy and the president could lead to a disrespectful, threatening barrage from the left.

How these pastors dared to leave the LWLP script to address crippling maladies that occur in distressed black communities with a sitting president who can use the power of the U.S. government to bring relief is a question the CBC, the NAACP, and BLM may be pulled into the woodshed to answer.

URBAN PROBLEM, RACISM'S FAULT

The *Chicago Tribune* reported a big drop in weekend violence in Chicago as only forty were shot. This number was down from the weekend before, when seventy-four were shot.

The *Tribune*'s Steve Chapman rejected what he calls the "popular myth, cynically promoted by Trump and other outside critics" that Chicago is an "exceptionally dangerous city."

Yes, 674 people were murdered last year in Chicago, more than in New York City and Los Angeles combined. But that is much better than 1991 when, says Chapman, 920 were murdered, and the total of 674 killed in 2017 was down 15 percent from 2016.

It's clear that violence in Chicago, and other urban areas, should concern us all—and particularly that it's largely a racial phenomenon.

As Chapman noted, "Chicago's crime problem is concentrated in a small number of poor, blighted, mostly African America neighborhoods."

But then he continued, "Those areas owe their plight largely to a sordid history of systematic, deliberate racial discrimination and violence, endemic poverty, and official neglect over the years."

For sure, misguided government policies have contributed to this sad state of affairs. But these policies were supposed to help these communities, not destroy them.

Policies such as government housing and excessive taxation that foster indifferent absentee landlords and crime-ridden blighted neighborhoods.

If there is any "deliberate racial discrimination" that has driven outsized violence and crime in black urban areas, it is the racial discrimination of the left. It is the racial discrimination of identity politics that promotes the idea that different ethnicities should live under different rules and receive special treatment.

Let's recall that the unfairness that blacks had to deal with in America's history was unequal treatment under the law. This is what needed to be fixed, and this is what was fixed by the Civil Rights Act in 1964.

The problem was that liberals wanted to use their agenda not to fix the law but to change the country. And, in the name of racial fairness, the era of big, activist government, financed with oceans of taxpayer funds, was born.

But government can't fix anybody's life. It can only make sure that the laws protecting life, liberty, and property are applied fairly and equally.

The beginning of big, activist government fostered the demise of personal responsibility.

The perpetrators and victims of violence in Chicago and other urban areas are largely young black men. They mostly come from homes with no father and from communities where this reality is the rule rather than the exception.

Making a child is not hard to do. Raising a child and conveying the values and rules that make for a successful life are, particularly in a nation where popular culture largely dismisses eternal truths and in black communities where politics and media are dominated by the left, who tell constituents that they suffer because of racism and that the answer is big government.

According to recent data from the Pew Research Center, 36 percent of black children under eighteen, compared with 74 percent of white children under eighteen, live in a household with married parents.

And, according to Pew, 30 percent of households headed by a single mother, 17 percent of households headed by a single father, 16 percent of households headed by an unmarried couple, and 8 percent of households headed by a married couple are poor.

Data from the Cook County Department of Health show that in 2016, 86 percent of babies born to black women between the ages of eighteen and twenty-nine were born outside marriage.

President Trump is doing his job. We have robust economic growth that we haven't seen in years with unemployment rates at record lows.

Congressional Black Caucus members and local black leadership need to start doing their job and convey that marriage, work, education, and personal responsibility are the only things that will fix black America.

It's in the interest of every African American to start thinking about their individual uniqueness and freedom again. It's in the interest of every African American to start dreaming again. This is what the civil rights movement was about.

Careful reasoning would shine light among black voters that it is in their interests that President Trump is an entrepreneurial, independent thinker who has the courage to fight against an entrenched status quo, including against CBC members that are standing in the way of progress.

Congresswoman Maxine Waters can threaten his cabinet from the rooftop, and he still won't stop. President Trump is a street fighter who has decided to fight for the little guy against the entrenched black left carnage-keepers. His passion to fix our nation's weakest neighborhoods is something African Americans need desperately.

The mistreatment of any and all blacks who disagree with liberals is well recorded, from athletes and actors to intellectuals and preachers. Post-Trump, not one conservative politician or pundit could escape the rage and wrath of the left. But, in the 2017 inaugural words of DJT, "...that is the past. And now we are looking only to the future."

PART FIVE

OPPORTUNITY
NOISE

CHAPTER THIRTEEN

Strong and Wealthy
and Alive Again

STRONG AGAIN

We will seek friendship and goodwill with the nations of the world—but we do so with the understanding that it is the right of all nations to put their own interests first. We do not seek to impose our way of life on anyone, but rather to let it shine as an example for everyone to follow.

—DJT Inaugural Address, 2017

I was privileged to attend the dedication of the new American embassy in Jerusalem on May 14, 2018—an event of enormous import that will remain with me forever. I am deeply grateful to America's Israeli Ambassador David Friedman and his wife, Tammy, for inviting me to this historic event.

The United States recognition of Jerusalem as Israel's capital is important not just for the United States and Israel but also for the entire world.

We might start thinking about this by considering the unique relationship between these two countries.

Regardless of how some choose to think about the United States today, the country's founding generation was largely Christian men and women.

Alexis de Tocqueville, author of *Democracy in America*, widely deemed to be the most insightful book ever written about the United States, wrote in 1835, "There is no country in the world where the Christian religion retains a greater influence over the souls of men than in America."

Perhaps there is no better example demonstrating this truth and the deep roots of Christian Americans' belief in the Hebrew Bible than the inscription on the Liberty Bell from the Book of Leviticus: "Proclaim liberty throughout all the land unto all inhabitants thereof."

The United States and Israel are different from other nations in that both are defined by a creed and by principles. And I would go as far as to say that the extraordinary success of both countries springs from these principles.

What are the great principles that can be extracted from the Ten Commandments in the Hebrew Bible?

Reverence for the Lord, reverence for family, reverence for the sanctity of life, reverence for private property and personal responsibility, and a prohibition of envy.

Some surely will say that the United States has strayed so far from these principles that they no longer define the country. But I travel constantly. I have been in every state of the union. And I have met enough of the many millions of Americans who still subscribe to these truths to know they are still very much alive in America.

And I also believe that the problems that plagued America in the past and that plague America today can be traced to abandonment of these great truths—these great truths rooted in the Hebrew Bible.

I see President Trump's courageous step forward to lead the United States to be the first nation in the world to recognize Jerusalem as the capital of the state of Israel and to move the U.S. Embassy to Jerusalem as implicit recognition that the common ground on which both nations stands is our shared belief in these great and holy truths.

The achievements of the young state of Israel, which celebrated its seventieth birthday in 2018, have been truly awesome.

Writer, social philosopher, investor, and my friend Dr. George Gilder wrote a book called *The Israel Test*.[18] What is the "Israel Test," according to Gilder? He asks the question: How do you react to those who exceed you in innovation, in creativity, in wealth? Do you envy them and feel diminished by them? Or do you admire what they have achieved and try to emulate them?

Those who say the latter pass the Israel Test. According to Gilder, it is the Israel Test that drives today's tensions in the Middle East. I would take it a step further and say that it is the Israel Test that drives the tensions in America.

At the root of tensions in both is a spirit of envy. Someone has something someone else doesn't have, and an entire political machinery is unleashed to take away from the haves and give to the have nots. And the haves fight back. This is the essence of the culture war.

Envy sums up the attacks in America against Christianity, capitalism, and our Constitution. Some folks just don't think it fair that some have much and others have little, and they ignore any reality that might explain why.

Gilder says that those who pass the Israel Test tend to become wealthy and peaceful. Those who fail it tend to become poor and violent.

The great principles that join America and Israel are equally true and crucial for all of mankind. And the number one principle is to admit that truth comes out of heaven, not out of one's head. The burden of American slavery exhibits a common denominator between Jews and American blacks: Jews attesting to God's existence and blacks attesting that man is not Him.

Making America truly strong again starts with this principle.

Congratulations to President Trump for helping America pass the Israel Test.

To declare to the world that America is strong enough to do the right thing even when everyone else is scared. That is leadership, and it is exactly what the world has missed as America went MIA while leading from behind.

Now we see the new forward-looking alliances gathering together around common visions of peace, prosperity, independent sovereignty, and freedom.

WEALTHY AGAIN

And whether a child is born in the urban sprawl of Detroit or the windswept plains of Nebraska, they look up at the same night sky, they fill their heart with the same dreams, and they are infused with the breath of life by the same almighty Creator.

—DJT Inaugural Address, 2017

Apple has become the first U.S. company in history to attain a trillion-dollar valuation. Here are a few thoughts about the relevance of this to our country and the world today.

The story of Apple is the story of Steve Jobs. He co-founded the company in 1976 at age twenty-one, was fired from the company he founded at age thirty, and then returned eleven years later, as it teetered on the edge of bankruptcy, to restore it and set it on the path to where it has arrived today.

First thing to think about is that Jobs was born in 1955. His biological mother, an unwed university graduate student, immediately put him up for adoption. This was eighteen years before abortion became legal in America by way of the *Roe v. Wade* decision.

If Jobs had been conceived eighteen years later or if *Roe v. Wade* had become law of the land eighteen years earlier, there is some chance that there never would have been a Steve Jobs. The life that would have become Steve Jobs could have been another in the vast sea of abortion statistics. There would be no Macs, iPods, or iPhones today.

The second thing worth thinking about is how vital freedom and capitalism are—not just to us but to the whole world.

By the end of the third quarter of 1997, when Jobs had returned to Apple, the company had lost more than a billion dollars, and by his estimate, it was within ninety days of insolvency.[19]

Jobs reviewed Apple's whole product line, and out of fifteen products, he eliminated eleven. Three thousand workers were immediately laid off. By 1998, Apple was once again profitable.

The key point is not just that Steve Jobs was a unique, driven, and extraordinarily gifted entrepreneur but also that he was free to act, to do what he thought needed to be done.

Once he regained control of the company, he was able to take full responsibility to assess the situation and take immediate steps to fix what he saw as broken.

Consider, in contrast, another trillion-dollar story.

The trillion-dollar budget deficits that the U.S. government faces now and into the near future.

Washington is filled with think tanks with all kinds of bright people analyzing and writing reports recommending what needs to be done to fix things. But these reports then go to politicians who can't—or won't—take action. We've got all kinds of recommendations, but no one can take charge, assume total responsibility, decide what to do, and do it.

Welfare programs and entitlement programs (many of which were designed fifty to eighty years ago) clearly don't work well and need to be redesigned or eliminated. Yet they go on and on, year after year after year.

It's the nature of the beast. We can't change what government is. But what we can do is limit its size and growth and maximize our private sector where freedom and capitalism can work.

It's important to think about this at a time when we're hearing so much, particularly from our young people, about how wonderful things would be with more government, more socialism.

Steve Jobs was committed to innovation—to "evolving, moving, refining"—all the time. More of our young people should be thinking about this while they're tweeting about socialism on their iPhones.

Surely, sentiments of America first, a country birthed in freedom to evolve, move, and refine, motivated many when they voted for a businessman to be in the White House. They wanted a tough guy who could say what needed to be done and say "you're fired" to those not performing.

But it's a lot harder in Washington. Most cannot be fired.

The system has been rigged in favor of a permanent, ruling bureaucracy immune from pressure from those who were merely elected or appointed as a result of that election.

The civil service system protects those who work for the people of the United States from being fired, which allows far too many to slow all business for the people. Name one government agency staffed with highly motivated workers who look to do their job expeditiously, effectively, and with a smile.

And now, we are finding out that some of these faceless bureaucrats bring their political interests to work and are attempting to wait out the president and his cabinet secretaries until they leave office simply by not doing their jobs, or, worse, a few are using their positions to try to destroy him.

The system was made dramatically worse under the Obama administration. The hiring process was changed by executive order to end the neutral application process where the first cut of résumés was made by computer evaluation and instead it added a simple résumé submission process.

This process allowed Obama's political appointees to choose their friends and philosophical allies for positions of importance and effectively ended the notion of the politically neutral civil service system.

An example of this new cronyism was uncovered at FEMA, the federal agency responsible for disaster recovery efforts.

The *New York Times* and *Washington Post* both reported that FEMA's chief component human capital officer (the head of personnel for those in the real world) abused the hiring process by giving his unqualified fraternity brothers jobs at the emergency response agency as well as hiring women he met from online dating sites. The women were then transferred to field offices with the intention that fraternity brothers could have sex with them.

While accusations of sexual misconduct against the FEMA hiring officer were rampant and he was temporarily moved out of his position on three different occasions, he somehow kept coming back to his old job.

Finally, in mid-2018, the offending high-ranking employee was fired from his $177,000 a year job, more than three years after the allegations of misconduct began to surface.

This story serves as a cautionary tale of the dangers of federal government employees who are virtually immune from firing being able to hire without regard for qualifications.

Far worse are the implications of public employee resister groups formed immediately upon the inauguration of President Trump, as these groups pledged to undermine President Trump's agenda.

They are hired as civil servants, get the security of permanent public employee positions, and then go on attack to attempt to bring the president's agenda down from the inside.

We already have a glimpse of the effects of what could happen if every department head in D.C. cannot drain their swamps of unqualified or unscrupulous staffers. Just review the incredible revelations about Justice Department and other personnel relating to the attempts to change the course of the 2016 presidential elections and undermine the sitting president of the United States.

There is practically nothing that can be accomplished by one person acting alone to drain the corruption inside the Beltway. The swamp is too deep and too dark.

But efforts are being made by some in Congress to restore their rightful Article One oversight authority and the power of the purse to root out government excesses and even defund the salaries of recalcitrant public employees.

Representative Tom Graves is leading a House Appropriations

Committee effort to change the focus of that committee from looking for ways to spend money to finding programs to defund with
modest success.

And while efforts to defund salaries have not yet succeeded, Representative Paul Gosar offered an amendment to a funding bill to
lower the salary of a high-ranking public employee who testified that
he wasn't going to follow orders from the executive branch.

While that effort also failed, it is a step in the right direction toward
Congress reasserting its rightful power to limit the size and scope of
government.

Therein lies the mission of the House Freedom Caucus.

The House Freedom Caucus is made up primarily of men and
women elected to office with entrepreneurial vision that together they
can get government within its boundaries set forth in the Constitution. A sort of *render to Caesar what's his and to God what's His* kind of
attitude. And it is in this attitude and direction for public policy that
American wealth will flourish.

To make America truly wealthy again starts with this kind of attitude but, more importantly, with focus, resolve, and patience.

ALIVE AGAIN

We are one nation—and their pain is our pain. Their dreams are our
dreams; and their success will be our success. We share one heart,
one home, and one glorious destiny. The oath of office I take today is
an oath of allegiance to all Americans.

—DJT Inaugural Address, 2017

Abortion starts with pain. Just the very thought of abortion starts
with a pregnancy. A pregnancy more often than not unplanned and
complicated. And most of life's times of complications and uncertainties are emotional and painful.

On abortion, the response of most societies throughout history was prohibition. The legal interruption of procreation was unthinkable, in consideration not just of morality but of human existence.

America legalized abortion on a national level in 1973 through the infamous *Roe v. Wade* decision, and our nation has been raging in culture war since.

Every year for the past twenty years, I have join the hundreds of thousands who arrive in Washington, D.C., for the annual March for Life, which notes the anniversary of the *Roe v. Wade* decision.

The march started in 1974 and will continue to take place every year until this disastrous and destructive decision is reversed.

Those who come to Washington express the breadth and depth of the resolve they hold for enshrining respect for the sanctity of life as part of our national culture. They often brave the hostile elements of winter in our nation's capital and have also braved many different political climates.

Upon the election of Donald Trump to the presidency, the pro-life political climate has dramatically improved, and major energy has been blown into the end abortion sails unlike any other political season since legalization. Most of these marchers of life believe that abortion is not salvation but a crime against humanity so America should not be doing it. I could feel the energy and excitement of the 2019 attendees toward our president and vice president as I participated in several of the March for Life events, including the ones hosted by my organization.

Operation Rescue, one of our country's leading pro-life Christian organizations historically known for chaining closed abortion clinic doors in the late eighties, named President Donald Trump the recipient of its 2018 Pro-Life Person of the Year award. This is noteworthy because OR is one of the most aggressive anti-abortion groups, evidenced by its graphic publicly displayed signs showing aborted babies. Momentum to revisit the national law of abortion is very high among the faithful, and Donald Trump is being given the credit.

America's political landscape is characterized by increased partisan polarization, as I have discussed throughout this book. Abortion is no exception. Far too many people have bought the lie that if it's legal, it's moral and are participating in abortion at unprecedented numbers, deepening the pain of the original pregnancy. Abortion is a horrific tragedy of heartbreaking and genocidal capacity. It's why the noise over abortion is grueling, emotionally personal, and violently intensified every time there is a Supreme Court vacancy.

Some concern of many pro-life and clergy leaders serving minority communities is that in addition to the moral implications of abortion and its mental and medical complications, abortion feeds into the narrative of victimhood. For liberals, abortion is a safety net of public policy, as if women have no control over their sexual impulses.

And blacks have been aggressively targeted by the left with messages of secularism and government safety nets to African Americans, those hardest hit by abortion. Black women constitute 6 percent of our population, yet they account for 35 percent of abortions. How can Democrats possibly be helping this community by supporting and encouraging this disaster?

It's vital for blacks, and for all Americans, to understand that abortion is not an issue to be viewed in isolation. Lack of respect for the sanctity of life spills over into other critical areas of human behavior.

It is no accident that the years since the *Roe v. Wade* decision have been years in which the American family has collapsed. In 1960, 73 percent of all children were living with two parents in a first marriage. By 2014, this was down to 46 percent. In 2014, 54 percent of black children were living with a single parent. Seventy-one percent of black babies were born to unwed mothers in 2014 compared with 20 percent in 1960. Research overwhelmingly shows the centrality of a healthy family structure to success in life. There is little question that the deep issues in black communities today tie to family collapse. And at the core of that collapse is the absence of reverence for the sanctity of life.

There is no issue more central to our national moral, physical, and fiscal health than abortion. And the partisan implications are clear.

Legal abortion is, at its core, about whether humanity growing in a womb should be included in what we consider mankind. If yes, it must be protected, like all life. The anti-abortion movement is clear on this. The unborn child is living and must be protected. If you believe the embryo is living, then life must be protected under the U.S. Constitution.

As the political left and the right move forward in our cultural battle for the heart and soul of America, fellow Americans should remember that although our Constitution was constructed by men, it was designed to protect and preserve principles from a higher place. Abortion is a symptom of and not the cause of the tensions, confusion, and noise in our nation. Our real problem is the abandonment of our society to the crass, gross ideas of an empty and false materialism that can only take us to oblivion.

> In America, we understand that a nation is only living as long as it is striving. We will no longer accept politicians who are all talk and no action—constantly complaining but never doing anything about it. The time for empty talk is over. Now arrives the hour of action.
>
> —DJT Inaugural Address, 2017

CHAPTER FOURTEEN

Proud and Safe and Growing Again

PROUD AGAIN

We've made other countries rich while the wealth, strength, and confidence of our country has disappeared over the horizon. One by one, the factories shuttered and left our shores, with not even a thought about the millions upon millions of American workers left behind.

—DJT Inaugural Address, 2017

In the wake of World War II, most of the industrialized world was destroyed. Germany was in ruins as was the rest of continental Europe, and Japan's manufacturing capacity had been significantly degraded.

Even Great Britain suffered immensely from the German bombing and missile attacks against its production capacity and populace.

The one exception was the United States, which escaped largely unscathed from the physical annihilation of war. Instead, the United States thrived economically during the war, developing its manufacturing capacity, to which many attributed the Allied victory.

After the war, various policies were developed to stave off the expansion of communism, including the Marshall Plan. Japan benefited from the necessity to reintegrate into the free world during the Korean War as it served as a supply depot for UN (largely made up of U.S.) forces.

Part of the United States and the Western world's efforts to keep the encroachment of communism at bay and grow the European and Japanese economies to offset the threat was to develop a world trading system wherein the United States would allow low-cost access to its markets yet keep protectionist policies in place elsewhere around the world.

This wealth redistribution effort solidified the United States as the dominant economic power in the world while growing Japan, Germany, Taiwan, and others as producers of goods for Americans to consume.

This world trading system, put into place in 1948, led to exponential growth of the world's economy and served as one of the guarantors of freedom.

When the Soviet Union fell, the trade system, which allowed newly vibrant Japan and Germany to compete with lower-cost labor and low tariffs, had achieved its mission.

In fact, it had gone beyond achieving its mission when the U.S. government had to bail out Chrysler Corporation in 1979 as rising gasoline prices and the shift in American tastes to the smaller vehicles that Japan and European manufacturers provided forced the smallest of the Big Three automakers to its knees.

The once-robust U.S. television and electronics industry was in tatters by the end of the 1980s, as famous nameplates like Thomas Edison's RCA began to become a thing of the past—doomed by a combination of Japanese currency manipulation, lower-cost overseas labor, and less-expensive imported products. The same unbalanced tariff system that had been designed to temporarily lift the world became an anchor around American manufacturers' collective necks.

It was time for the system to be rebalanced to provide for trade rules more favorable to the United States, but no one in the world was feeling sorry for the largest economy in the world, and the United

States was not interested in standing up for itself, hoping the lower prices due to exporting labor costs would provide a long-term offset.

President Trump was elected with the promise that he would rebalance the system to get out of what had become "bad, bad deals," which always were intended to disadvantage America and her workers—and these workers had had enough.

After President Bill Clinton gave China access to our markets by granting it permanent normalized trade relations and he signed NAFTA, American factories began to shutter and leave our shores. Workers were getting crushed. Welfare and food stamp rolls began to creep back to 1996 numbers.

Trade deals that had hollowed out the United States manufacturing core threatened to end our nation's ability to produce the high-grade steel needed to build military equipment.

President Trump interrupted the new normal, in which far too many Americans simply accepted trading their long-term economic security for lower-cost widgets.

On top of the trade equity imbalance, the United States maintained the highest tax rate on businesses in the industrialized world, discouraging domestic investment as part of the outdated trade policy of exporting U.S. wealth to help the rest of the world grow.

Detroit, Michigan, once the symbol of U.S. industrial might, suffered egregiously through deindustrialization. Trade and union policy motivated its population to flee by almost two-thirds, creating urban blight and exacerbating all of the social ills that go with sudden migration.

However, all that changed when President Trump made America's economic security his national priority.

Suddenly, the Trans-Pacific Partnership (TPP), which locked the United States into the role of blood donor nation for the rest of the world even as the patient was running low on the precious fluid, would be a thing of the past.

When trade agreements with South Korea and NAFTA were renegotiated, the president argued for fair and reciprocal trade deals designed to create the exact rebalancing of the seventy-year-old world trade order, and manufacturing began to come back to America.

Steel plants reopened, and the European Union agreed on pursuing a pathway to reciprocal reductions of industrial, non-auto trade down to 0 percent on both sides of the Atlantic. With President Trump in office just under two years, American blue-collar workers started feeling economically proud again.

SAFE AGAIN

When America is united, America is totally unstoppable. There should be no fear—we are protected, and we will always be protected. We will be protected by the great men and women of our military and law enforcement and, most importantly, we are protected by God.

—DJT Inaugural Address, 2017

Economic security is not complete without moral security, and America is literally left naked in this area. Our culture has let down its moral guardrails, and people are very afraid.

A *Washington Post* story was captioned, "I warned him: woman, 68, shoots man doing private thing on bike who then chased her to her doorstep."

Private thing?

It's exactly what folks on the right have been trying to say about all sexual matters: that these matters are adult and private, so what will result from us exposing kindergarteners to them?

The *Washington Post* reported, "The sign on her door reportedly said, 'Save the drama for your mama.' But when that message didn't appear to get across to the man masturbating on her doorstep, the sixty-eight-year-old Houston woman warned that she would have to get her pistol."

The woman, identified only as "Granny Jean" in local news, was taking out her trash early one evening when the man riding his bicycle while involved in a sexual act approached her, according to Houston police.

"Some guy pulled off his pants and pulled his pants open, playing with his thing," she told the local ABC affiliate, "and he ran up in my yard, and I told him to get away from my door, or I will shoot him." He didn't stop approaching, and the woman's fourteen-year-old granddaughter was inside the house, so she grabbed her gun and shot him through the door.

He is expected to survive his injuries, but there are countless incidents like this all across America since our society has relaxed its public policy regarding sexual matters. And it's just not safe for anybody to have uncertainty in laws that govern sexual matters.

What a lot of American information bystanders/voters don't realize is how much America has changed. Since the legalization of same-sex marriage, every family law in the country is being debated or has already been rewritten from adoption law to age of consent law to retirement law. All federal laws and state laws regarding education and prisons, religious liberty, and public nudity or decency are under scrutiny in search of nondiscrimination compliance.

What does a state do with a transvestite criminal who hasn't had surgery?

How do our public schools accommodate seven-year-old children who are questioning their gender identification? Should it be legal or illegal for an Uber driver to refuse customers who are passionately petting in their car? Should there be any prequalification for folks seeking to foster or adopt children in our foster system, and if so, what should those guidelines be?

Throughout our history, safety concerns have driven U.S. policy regarding children. But all of that changed in 2015 when the U.S. Supreme Court ruled in favor of same-sex marriage as the law of the land. Now, lawsuits related to this new reality abound in an attempt to relax public policy over adopting, teaching, scouting, showering, and bathrooms.

With Trump using his bully pulpit as a law-and-order president, it's easy for one to think this the only aspect of his declaration to make America safe again. But there's little on the news that makes adult hearts beat faster than when children are at safety risk.

Whether trapped in a cave in the Philippines or in a boat fleeing a war-torn country or crying at our own border with Mexico, children in peril always stir the emotions of most adults.

But for some adults, children are prey. Some adults abuse and torment children. Some adults rape and torture children. So, most civilized societies have established impenetrable laws to protect children first and foremost and America had some of the strictest protections.

American children of the twenty-first century should not be subjected to mental or physical danger simply because some adults want to be more public on sexual matters. Yet this is where the country is. It's yet another reason Trump is president.

With President Trump in the driver's seat as our country sorts through these new questions regarding children and as more and more unbridled sexual passions are expressed publicly, many are confident that the emperor will soon be wearing clothes again.

GROWTH AGAIN

A new national pride will stir our souls, lift our sights, and heal our divisions. It is time to remember that old wisdom our soldiers will never forget: that whether we are black or brown or white, we all bleed the same red blood of patriots, we all enjoy the same glorious freedoms, and we all salute the same great American Flag.

—DJT Inaugural Address, 2017

When I read that the economy is growing strongly, it makes me happy. But in politics, good news is not enough. You have to decide who gets credit for it.

President Ronald Reagan, no ordinary politician, kept a plaque on his desk that said, "There is no limit to what a man can do or where he can go if he does not mind who gets the credit."

Nevertheless, a good deal of the discussion surrounding the news that the economy grew hugely within even eighteen months of Trump's leadership was about how much credit President Donald Trump deserved.

Paul Krugman, the very left-wing Nobel prize–winning economist, for whom there is nothing Trump can do that is good for the American people, dismissed this great economic news in his *New York Times* column, calling it a "nothing burger."[20]

I think it's more than a nothing burger to the many finding their way back into the workforce because of a brisk economy growing at a pace we haven't seen in a decade.

The *Wall Street Journal* reported that "Americans looking to land a first job or break into a dream career face their best odds of success in years."[21]

According to the report, companies trying to hire in a labor market are loosening the requirements that they once sought in job applicants. Relaxed work requirements put 1.2 million jobs in closer reach to more applicants, per the *Wall Street Journal*.

President Trump campaigned on the promise that his administration would provide hope to those forgotten Americans who had been left behind in the "new normal" economy. Eighteen months into his presidency, the number of unemployed Americans dropped to the second-lowest level since 9/11, even as the noninstitutionalized population increased by 43 million in that same time.

Even more interesting is that the number of people ages sixteen to sixty-four not in the workforce decreased by 2.7 million, even as the overall population of that working-age population increased by 1 million. That's 3.7 million more people, most of whom had given up on the American dream, reenlisting in the economy.

The forgotten are forgotten no more, not because of handouts but because of lower taxes, less regulation, and a rational, "America first" vision from President Trump.

Now this same Krugman wrote another piece in the *New York Times*: "The G.O.P.'s War on the Poor." Krugman was unhappy about

Republican proposals to add work requirements to welfare programs like Medicaid. Which, I think, is a great idea.

But the point here is that the best answer for those on welfare who can work is a job. And that the best anti-poverty program is a growing, robust economy. More jobs and opportunity are the "nothing burger" now being served up to millions of Americans.

There is this question among the chattering class, especially the never-Trumpers, about how much credit Trump and the Republican Congress can take for this incredible growth in such a short time span.

We know what Krugman thinks about who should get credit for America growing again. But there are more distinguished economists who share with Trump the conviction that the economy is recovering because of the tax cuts and deregulation measures put in place in the first year of his presidency.

It is worth looking at the *Economic Freedom of the World Index*, published annually by the Fraser Institute in Vancouver, Canada. The index measures economic freedom in 159 countries around the world, using forty-two different parameters.

The index is important because it correlates extremely strongly with economic growth. Countries that score the best grow the fastest.

In 2000, the United States was fourth out of 159 countries. By 2014, the United States had dropped to fourteenth. Scores regarding the size of our government, our legal system, and business regulation all deteriorated. This correlated with the slowdown in growth and the very slow economic recovery.

These are all the areas that Trump is fixing. So, it's no surprise that the economy is recovering due to the Trump administration.

I don't have a Nobel Prize in economics, but I'm ready to give President Trump and Republicans the credit. Contrary to a GOP "war on the poor," I'd say that, with an abundance of new jobs and historically low unemployment rates for blacks and Hispanics, the GOP is leading a new economic renaissance for the poor and all working Americans.

Tax reform lowered taxes for most Americans but most importantly ended the U.S. status as having the highest corporate tax rate
in the industrialized world, ending the financial incentives to export
manufacturing jobs overseas while selling the products to American
consumers.

The trillions of dollars that American corporations made overseas
but did not reinvest in the United States due to the high taxes began
to come home by the hundreds of millions to expand and upgrade
facilities, pay dividends, give wage increases, invest in more research,
and even increase stock prices, helping pension funds dependent
upon a rising stock market to meet their obligations.

Employment rates for African Americans, Hispanics, and people
with disabilities grew to all-time-high levels, as the need for labor and
profits pierced any actual or perceived biases, creating opportunity
for all.

Donald Trump won his presidency not because of the black, Hispanic, or disability vote but by unleashing the power of America's free
enterprise system, and it is these exact voters who will have gained the
most by virtue of his presidency.

Unbinding America's capitalist engine from the chains of politics
gone bad, high taxes, and strangling, unnecessary regulations is just
the beginning of economic vibrancy that truly gives economic hope
to all.

The same tax bill that encouraged trillions to be privately rein-
vested in America provided additional incentives for investments
to be made in America's most distressed zip codes. This is positive
movement that hopefully will not be stopped by the LWLPs driving
Trump supporters underground.

Inclusion has to first and foremost mean the ability to get a job,
chase your dream, and have the opportunity to catch it. More than
ever before, everyone is being included in the workforce because capitalism is color, gender, and disability blind, only caring about who can
help make or provide things at a cost that others are willing to pay.

Ultimately, opportunity noise is about helping people understand that unleashing Christianity, capitalism, and our Constitution so people are no longer slaves to a welfare state and have the dignity of work and self-determination is the only moral choice. Wages grow one step up the job or business ladder at a time.

Those who have led us to believe that the velvet handcuffs of ever-expanding government social programs are righteous have to face the reality that only the moral guidelines of Christianity, the virtue of capitalism, and the stability of our Constitution can lift all boats to opportunities of personal peace and prosperity while socialism seeks to lower everyone to common poverty.

America has a stark choice. Expand a new socialist normal of accepting the downward spiral of American pride, child safety, and economic growth in exchange for the comfortable chains of government handouts or look forward to the noisy bumps that come with an eight-year Donald J. Trump presidency.

King Solomon said in Ecclesiastes 7:12 (NKJV) that "…the excellency of knowledge is that wisdom gives life to those who have it." And I believe that in that life we can be assured by the excellency of knowledge that freedom always beats slavery.

> Finally, we must think big and dream even bigger. Do not let anyone tell you it cannot be done. No challenge can match the heart and fight and spirit of America. We will not fail. Our country will thrive and prosper again.
>
> —DJT Inaugural Address, 2017

CHAPTER FIFTEEN

KAG Dreaming

IN THIS final chapter of *Necessary Noise*, the question left before us is where we go from here.

Sadly, too much of America's recent history has us percolating in a world of uncertainty as we have lost clarity about what our nation is about, what our common goals are, and what they mean. We have been merely twisting and turning, almost randomly, toward some unknown and unclear destination. If there is any unifying characteristic of recent times, it can only be summed up as materialism.

I don't just mean love of material things: a bigger house, a fancier car, and more expensive clothes, jewelry, and vacations. I mean a sense that money is the answer to everything and that everything worthwhile can be bought. It is a belief that with money, life's uncertainties can be eliminated and peace and paradise can be acquired.

Just a glance at the increasing percentage of our national economy that is allocated to government spending tells this story.

In 1900, federal government spending consumed a little less than 3 percent of our national economy. By 2018, this increased to 21 percent. Add in spending at the state and local government levels and total government spending in 1900 was a little less than 8 percent of the national economy. By 2018, it was 32 percent. One out of every three dollars that our economy produces is taken by government.

And we get more of a sense of what is going on by seeing how federal government spending has changed. In 1952, 70 percent of federal government spending was defense spending, and 15 percent was transfer payments, which is government taxing and spending the money on other citizens. By 2013, this was totally reversed. About 20 percent of federal spending was for defense, and 70 percent was for transfer payments.

What's the makeup of this 70 percent of federal spending in transfer payments to individuals? Almost 40 percent is government health care spending—Medicare, Medicaid, and Obamacare. Another third is Social Security. And 20 percent is anti-poverty programs. Around 5 percent is spending for veterans.

What all of this means is that once—back in the 1950s—our view of most of the job of the federal government was to pay for our national defense. Now we have totally changed our view of what government is for. Our view now is that it's the government's job to take care of our health care, to take care of our retirement, to fight poverty, and to generally help out citizens who are having a hard time in life. In other words, once upon a time America was about living free. We took care of ourselves and gave up some of what we produced and earned to pay our government to protect us from threats from abroad. Living free meant everyone taking responsibility for themselves and their life.

By giving up our freedom and along with it our personal responsibility under the illusion that government spending can solve all our problems, we wind up on the path to bankruptcy in a public square culture war over who gets to spend the taxes and on what.

One of my colleagues at CURE and I regularly banter about who first coined the phrase "I've never seen someone wash a rented car." But who first said it matters less than the truth in it: that people take care of what belongs to them. When you think somebody else can or should solve your problems, the result is just waste and inefficiency.

And, indeed, this is what is happening to our culture and our country. We are bankrupting ourselves by relinquishing our freedom.

The federal budget is in deficit approaching $1 trillion. The Congressional Budget Office projects these trillion-dollar deficits as far as the eye can see. As a result, our total nation debt burden keeps increasing. In 1980, federal debt as a percent of GDP was 35 percent. In 2001, it was 54 percent. Now it is approaches 100 percent.

America's impending debt crisis could bring down the whole house. We cannot afford to go on like this. It is like a kind of drug addiction. The addicted person keeps spending more and more, relinquishing more of his personal freedom, personal integrity, and personal responsibility under the illusion that a substance will solve his problems. We have been slowly, step-by-step, year after year relinquishing our freedom by thinking that our life needs can be purchased and provided for by the government.

RENEWING OUR FAITH

It's no accident that coinciding with this new materialistic and economic worldview has been a dramatic drop in religious faith. According to Gallup, in 1957 82 percent of Americans said that religion "can answer all or most of today's problems." By 2017, this was down to 55 percent. The less America goes to church, the more dependent we become on the government. Faith becomes replaced with fear, and over the years Uncle Sam has become our soother.

Therefore, it is imperative that there is a renewal of our faith in order to restore vitality to our nation and deal with enormous fiscal problems. We must restore clarity that America is about individual freedom. When this becomes clear, then along with this it becomes clear that we can restore control and responsibility to every citizen for their own life, their own being.

RESTORING OUR RESPONSIBILITY

One of the first lessons we see in the Bible is of property rights. God told Adam that is yours and this is mine.

In order for America to regain itself, the first order of business is to separate from government everything unique individuals should be doing. We must go program by program, reforming and reinventing.

Mountains of data and blocks of dirty streets show the fruitlessness of secularism and government dependency. It is disingenuous that we pretend to care about the poor yet we allow our taxes to be spent on programs we know are trapping them in lives of despair. The steps out of poverty are not rocket science. Yet people need to be free to take them, and there is no freedom in government dependency.

Promising ideas abound on how to redirect government policies that can empower rather than debilitate personal freedom and the human spirit: parental choice in schools, vouchers to acquire housing flexibility or private health insurance, tax-free zip code zones, and charity tax credits, to name only a few.

I have worked for years to transform Social Security to a program of individually owned personal retirement accounts. Why not allow our nation's youth to redirect their payroll taxes away from the IRS and into an IRA?

Once we refocus on goals of freedom and individual responsibility, everything else will fall into place, and we'll know what to do.

CLOSING ARGUMENT FOR FREEDOM

President Donald Trump promised to make America great again, and many of those who oppose him claim America never was great. That is the battle for the DNA of America.

There is no doubt that America has bred and imported an enemy within, like a cancer corrupting the body, sowing self-doubt about our very survival. The challenges to America's DNA of individual liberty protected by government, rather than granted by government, are real. But America can emerge stronger if we rededicate ourselves to the principles of freedom after a long-overdue discussion, indeed a political fight, over what America means.

The allure of freedom is so strong that it attracts those who desire it like bees to a flower in bloom. And now we have the generational chance to flex our muscles by providing a robust defense of individual liberty to those for whom our systems have failed to define it. However, it is not enough to offer platitudes of the past to many Americans, new and old, to whom these words have become stale. It is my hope that this book has provided you with insight about the origins of the debate and some of the deep challenges ahead.

Most Americans are a *roll up our sleeves and get it done* kind of people. One of the vibrant aspects of our national character is to fix a problem ourselves rather than waiting around for someone else or the government to do it. This translates to the local church-run food banks that provide not only the physical but also the spiritual nourishment we all need when troubles come our way. It is the local business that hires the kid who hangs around outside to help in the stockroom, putting that kid on the pathway of the hope and dignity of a job.

And the parent who volunteers in their kid's school and becomes a mentor to other kids whose parents may be out of the picture. Remember that for every millennial wearing the all-black of Antifa trying to disrupt or intimidate a Trump supporter, there are a thousand who are voluntarily serving in our military doing the impossible in the most inhospitable environments.

For every millennial who falls into tears over even hearing Donald Trump's name, there are a hundred working in the oil fields, construction sites, and manufacturing plants that are being revived all over America. For the few thousands marching in a gay pride Saturday event to divide us, there are 100 million American families going into their local church on Sunday.

The happy truth is that millennials want to participate in the American dream, and when the chance to do so arises, they seize that new opportunity. The happy truth is that most people participating in morally questionable lifestyles get up and go to work everyday with the intention to be their best professional selves.

And while many of them have been taught that wearing a Che

Guevara T-shirt is cool and associate socialism with the butterflies, unicorns, and rainbows reminiscent of John Lennon's song "Imagine," when the rubber meets the road, they want to make their own lives without government telling them what to do.

Most Americans of all backgrounds, ethnicities, and political or personal choices believe in equality. The question is whether we will fall prey to the sophistry of those who preach equality of outcomes or the excitement of equality of opportunity where each of us can try, succeed, or fail to reach our dreams.

And when we fall short, we get the opportunity to pick ourselves up and try again.

It is up to freedom-lovers to share truth with them, to show them what God's love looks like, and to provide the best defense of a free capitalist society where our rights come from our Creator.

America is not perfect. While being conceived in liberty, it was founded by men who were not demigods sent down from Mount Olympus but people with their own struggles and flaws.

Those who wish to destroy our nation choose to focus on the flaws while ignoring the aspirations and higher ideals that make our nation unique in the world.

The choice is simple. Either we will embrace the American ideal and continue to strive toward freedom, or our nation will sink into the scrap heap of history, to be examined in a thousand years like Athens or Rome in order to determine why we traded freedom for the false sense of security offered by totalitarianism.

Rick and I believe in our nation's future. One of the great strengths and dangers of our nation is that we always have a choice of whether to embrace the freedom to fail without a government net.

The decision of whether to reelect Donald Trump will be one of those seminal moments where the choice will be stark. This is our time to make the case for freedom.

And, God willing, it is the chance for America to turn away from the scourge of collectivism.

Members of the left are fond of the Marxist presumption that they are on the right side of history, but in America, we get to determine what our future and hence our history will be. And settling our cultural war will mean that we will battle in the voting booth every two, four, and six years. Some vote for freedom, some for government control.

We choose freedom.

Thus, we hope that *Necessary Noise* has clarified some of the challenges and the choices to inspire you to join us in making the necessary noise and that the irresistible call and promise of freedom will ring loudly enough that it is heard not only here in America but across the world.

Acknowledgments

RICHARD MANNING (first to say good idea!). He started writing down everything I would say out loud in his company, and then some; so I started writing and writing and after two weeks we knew that I'd better call my agent!

Many thanks to my agent Eric Wolgemuth and the Agency of Wolgemuth and Associates, the bench from where Robert Wolgemuth would annually call to see if a book was stirring inside me.

And the winner Publisher is Center Street! Many thanks to my first editor Virginia, who then handed me off to Sean. What a wonderful team that made my job incredibly easy to simply meet the deadlines. Oh and to creative, the cover design is awesome.

Thanks also to my inner circle, Bob Borens my best friend, Jackie Cissell my best confidant, and Clint Gillespie my best comrade.

And to my CURE team, for keeping CURE programs moving while I was writing for three straight months.

A task I also could not have done without my CURE family of donors, from my very precious Presidents Circle members, my faithful Gold and Silver members, to my dedicated Club 100s and my Rising Stars!

Oh and my CURE Board, with big shout-outs to John and Judy for their endless encouragement, and Marc and Tegra for consistent care. Dr. Bill Allen who lets me brainstorm thoughts no matter what time of day nor how trivial of analyses, and to Angela and Ginni my dear friends who just love me.

Endnotes

1. https://www.chicagotribune.com/news/local/breaking/ct-transgender -palatine-high-school-lawsuit-met-20160504-story.html
2. *N.Y. Times,* June 1, 2015; Reuters, June 1, 2015; *WSJ,* June 2, 2015
3. TheBecketFund.org, September 27, 2013; U.S.News.com, January 9, 2014
4. WashingtonPost.com, March 26, 2013; L.A.Times.com, April 21, 2014
5. Courtlistener.com, *Dixon v. University of Toledo,* 638 F. Supp. 2d, 847 (N.D. Ohio 2009)
6. *Welfare Reformed: A Compassionate Approach*; Theologian R. C. Sproul of Ligonier, Statism, page 57, Legacy Communications 1994
7. Inc.com, Justin Bariso, July 26, 2017; Bloomberg.com, Brad Stone, October 6, 2011
8. goacta.org, 2011, 2015, 2017
9. Quotes.net
10. CBS News, March 28, 2018
11. Dr. Judith Reisman, *Sexual Sabotage: How One Mad Scientist Unleashed a Plague of Corruption and Contagion on America* (Washington, DC: WND Books, 2010), 134.
12. Numbersofabortions.com; Lifenews.com
13. CNN health, by Nancy Coleman, CNN, August 1, 2017
14. *Psychology Today*, October 12, 2017, Katherine Schreiber and Heather Hausemblas, Why Are Suicide Rates Higher among LGBTQ Youth?
15. Williams Institute Law; UCLA.edu; transequality.org
16. Kelvin Cochran, *Who Told You That You Were Naked?* (3G Publishing, Inc, 2013).

17. Congressional Black Caucus, cbc.house.gov, January 19, 2017, Letter to DJT

18. George Gilder, *The Israel Test: Why the World's Most Besieged State Is a Beacon of Freedom and Hope for the World Economy* (Richard Vigilante Books, 2009), 234.

19. Inc.com, Justin Bariso, July 26, 2017; Bloomberg.com, Brad Stone, October 6,2011

20. *N.Y. Times*, CNN, Paul Krugman on Trump Tax Cuts, May, 2, 2018

21. *WSJ*, July 28, 2018.

Index

About the Authors

STAR PARKER is an author and conservative thought leader. She is the founder and president of the Center for Urban Renewal and Education (UrbanCURE), which she started after consulting on federal welfare reform in the 1990s. Star is a frequent television commentator regularly seen on *Fox & Friends* and *The Sean Hannity Show*. She lives in Washington, DC.

RICHARD MANNING is a graduate of the University of Southern California. His career in politics and policy includes working for the federal government and running a DC-based interest group that specializes in grassroots marketing. Today, as president of Americans for Limited Government, he is heard weekly in over 100 radio markets giving "Swamp Updates," is a co-host on *Breitbart News Tonight* on SiriusXM 125, and frequently guests on One America News Network. Rick is married and involved in youth ministry at his local church.